my first
craft book

my first craft book

Over 35 fun projects for children aged 7–11 years old

Edited by Susan Akass

CICO **kidz**

Published in 2011 by CICO Kidz
An imprint of Ryland Peters & Small
519 Broadway, 5th Floor,
New York NY 10012
20–21 Jockey's Fields,
London WC1R 4BW

www.cicobooks.com

10 9 8 7 6 5 4 3 2

A CIP catalog record for this book is
available from the Library of Congress
and the British Library.

ISBN: 978-1-907563-34-8

Printed in China

Editor: Susan Akass
Designer: Elizabeth Healey
Illustration: Hannah George
See page 128 for photography credits.

For digital editions, visit
www.cicobooks.com/apps.php

Contents

Introduction

If you are reading this, then you are probably someone who loves to make things and is looking for new ideas. This book is full of them!

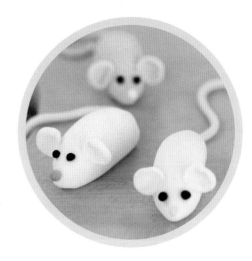

My First Craft Book is divided into six chapters to pick and choose from. The Holiday Fun section is for celebration days—Easter, Halloween, and Christmas—with gifts and decorations to make. There is a Creative Costumes section, to inspire you for fancy dress or make believe games. Plus, there are chapters on Simple Sewing, Papercrafting, and Natural Materials, with heaps of great things to have a go at making. You can even try some basic recipes in the Baking and Sugarcraft chapter. Some of the projects are very easy and use materials you can find around your house. For others, you will need to plan ahead and buy some special materials, but it will be worth it because of the lovely things you will be able to create.

To help you, we have graded all the projects with one, two, or three smiley faces. The grade one projects are the easiest, and these can be made with materials from your craft box. The grade two projects require some special materials, which you will probably have to buy. The grade three projects require special materials and some help from a willing adult.

These are easy projects that can be made with craft-box materials.

These projects require some special materials.

These projects require special materials and help from an adult.

You will need:

☆☆☆☆☆☆☆☆☆☆☆☆☆☆☆

For all projects, you will need some basic craft materials. We suggest your craft box should include:

pencils
a ruler
a set square
a sharpener
an eraser
white paper
thin card
fine felt-tipped pens
acrylic paints
wide and fine paint brushes
a pair of sharp scissors
a glue stick
a pot of PVA glue
needles
thread
floss (embroidery thread)

It is also a good idea to collect materials you may need, especially different patterned wrapping papers, tissue paper, ribbons, fabric scraps, wool scraps, felt scraps, buttons, pipe cleaners, beads, and toothpicks.

Remember

Remember to wear an apron when you work with paint or glue and to cover work surfaces with some old newspaper. Have fun! When you have finished a project, give it to someone as a gift, wear it, or display it somewhere wonderful and then stand back and say proudly, "I made that!"

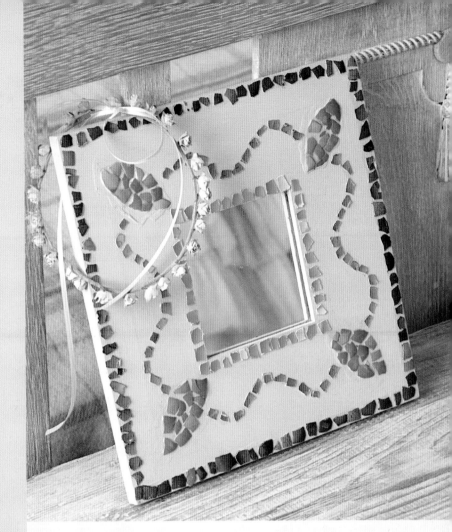

Chapter 1

Papercrafting

cupcake toppers

These little toppers are easy to make and add a colorful touch to party cupcakes. Instead of boats, you could try making other shapes such as football shirts or little ghosts for Halloween. You could even write names on the toppers and use them as place markers at your party.

You will need:

★★★★★★★★★★★★

Topper templates (page 125)

Paper and a pencil to make paper pattern shapes

Scissors

A piece of card (you could use an old cereal packet)

Scraps of colored paper

A glue stick

Toothpicks

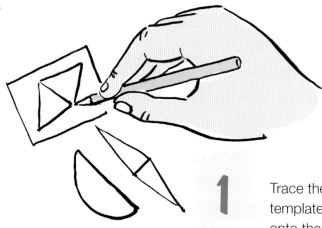

1 Trace the topper templates on page 125 onto the paper. Cut them out and draw around them on some card. Cut out these shapes and you will have three strong templates which you can draw around lots of times onto different-colored papers. Cut out a flag, a sail, and two boat pieces for each topper.

2 Fold the flag and sail shapes in half. Spread glue on the inside. Stick the flag and sail at the top of the toothpick, with the toothpick between the folded layers.

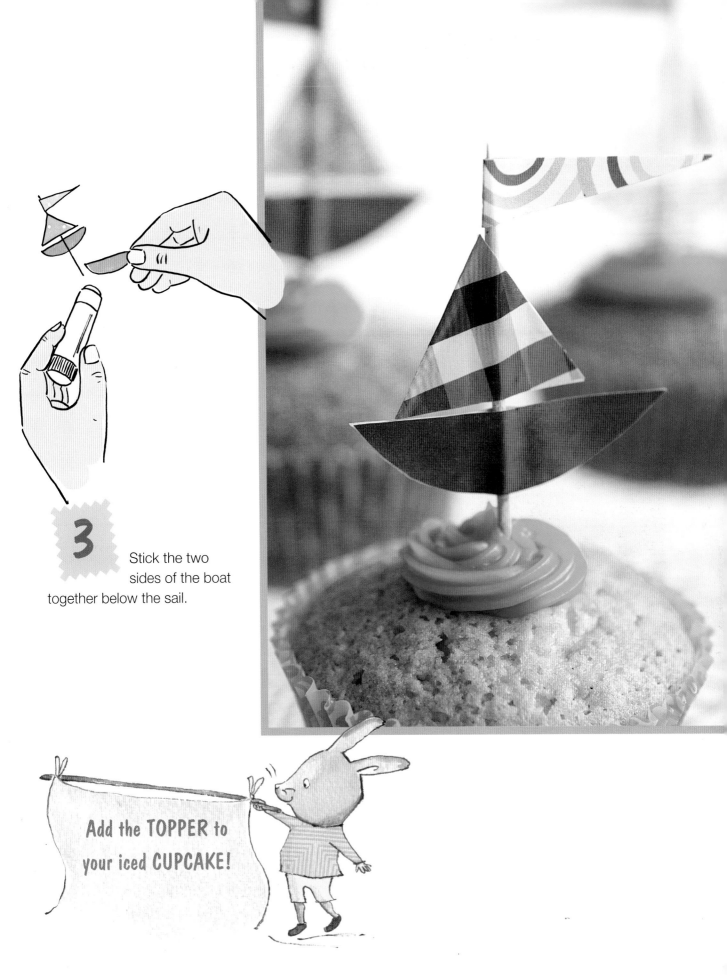

3 Stick the two sides of the boat together below the sail.

Add the TOPPER to your iced CUPCAKE!

glitter star card

A card that doesn't need an envelope—an exciting, glittery surprise to arrive in the mail at the house of your best friend, aunt, or grandma! Just fold the flaps, seal with a glittery dot, and your card is ready to be sent.

You will need:

Star template (page 15)

White paper

A pencil

Scissors

Scrap paper

A small coin

PVA glue

Glitter in a similar color to the card

Thin colored card

Silver paper

A glue stick

1 Trace the star template on page 15 onto the paper and cut it out carefully. On a scrap of spare paper, draw around a small coin and cut this circle out too.

2 Cover the star and the circle with a thin layer of PVA glue. Put them on some scrap paper and sprinkle over the glitter until they are covered. Shake any glitter that has not stuck off onto the scrap paper and pour it back into the pot. Let the shapes dry.

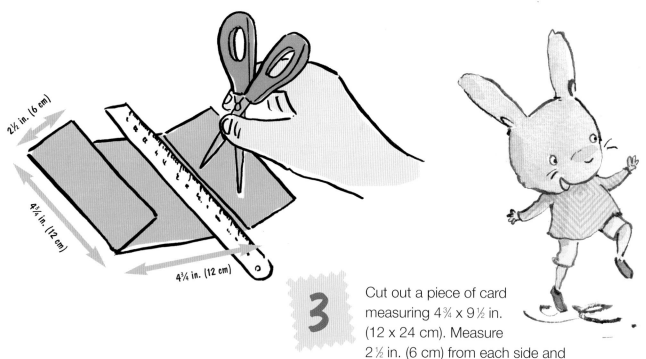

2½ in. (6 cm)

4¾ in. (12 cm)

4¾ in. (12 cm)

3 Cut out a piece of card measuring 4¾ x 9½ in. (12 x 24 cm). Measure 2½ in. (6 cm) from each side and score gently with the point of the scissors. Fold the card along the score lines so that the two sides fold into the center.

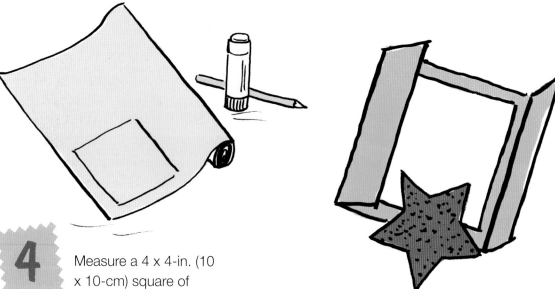

4 Measure a 4 x 4-in. (10 x 10-cm) square of silver paper. Cut it out and stick it inside the card using the glue stick.

5 Use some more PVA glue to stick the star into the center of the square.

Everyone LOVES a HOMEMADE card.

6 Write your greeting inside one of the side flaps. Close the flaps over the star.

7 Using a little glue from the glue stick, stick the glitter circle across the two flaps to hold them closed. The circle will pull off easily to open the card. Write the name and address on the back of the card and it is ready for posting.

Star template—shown at actual size (100%)

SEND the card to a special FRIEND or one of your relatives!

papier-mâché bowl

Do you like getting covered in goo? Here's your chance! Make a beautiful papier-mâché bowl using newspaper and glue. Remember to cover your work surface with newspaper before you start and to wear an apron for this wonderfully messy project.

You will need:

2 plastic bowls

Petroleum jelly (Vaseline)

Plastic wrap (cling film)

Newspaper

PVA glue

Water

Scissors

Matt latex (household emulsion) or acrylic paint

A wide paint brush

Scraps of wrapping paper

1 Smear the underside of one plastic bowl with a layer of petroleum jelly. Now cover it with a piece of plastic wrap (cling film).

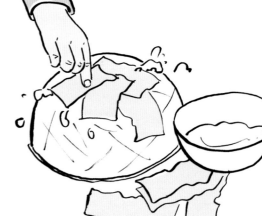

2 Tear some newspaper into strips. Small strips will give your bowl a smoother finish.

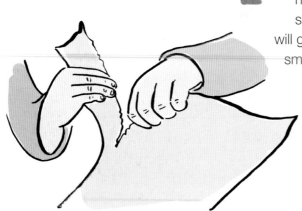

3 Pour PVA glue into the other plastic bowl. Add water, a little at a time, and stir until the glue is like runny paint. Dip pieces of newspaper into the glue and start to paste them over the plastic wrap. Keep pasting pieces until the bowl is covered with at least three layers of paper.

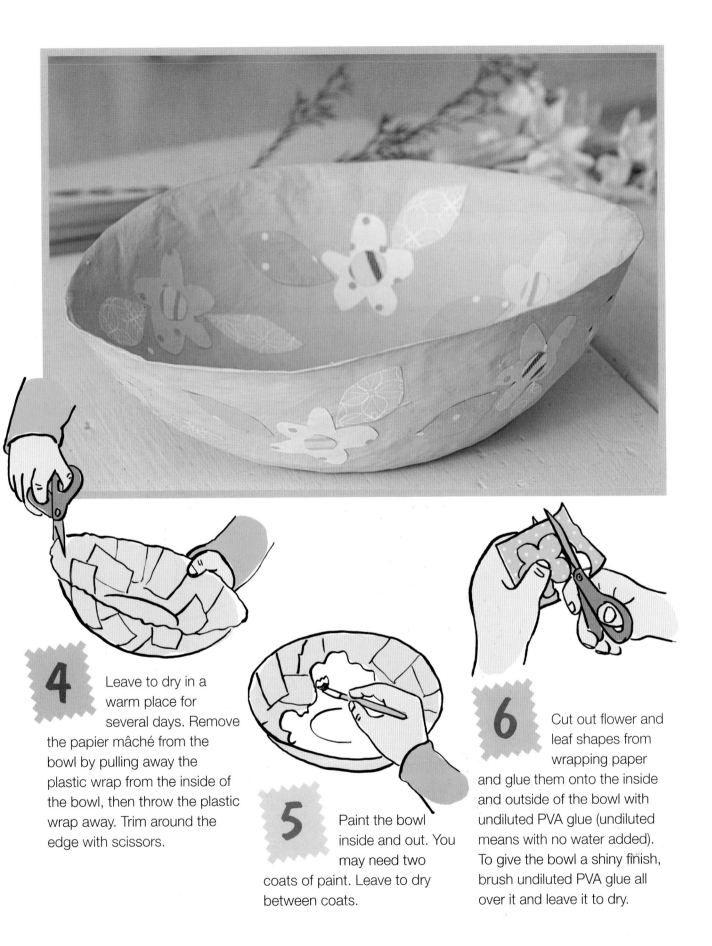

4 Leave to dry in a warm place for several days. Remove the papier mâché from the bowl by pulling away the plastic wrap from the inside of the bowl, then throw the plastic wrap away. Trim around the edge with scissors.

5 Paint the bowl inside and out. You may need two coats of paint. Leave to dry between coats.

6 Cut out flower and leaf shapes from wrapping paper and glue them onto the inside and outside of the bowl with undiluted PVA glue (undiluted means with no water added). To give the bowl a shiny finish, brush undiluted PVA glue all over it and leave it to dry.

inu (origami dog)

Your friends will love these adorable, floppy eared, paper puppies and you can quickly learn to make them using small pieces of paper. After you have folded the paper, create your own puppy character by drawing on eyes and whiskers. When you are good at it, you can use large pieces of paper to make dog masks for fancy dress parties.

You will need:

☆☆☆☆☆☆☆☆☆☆

6 x 6-in. (15 x 15-cm) square piece of paper

A marker pen or stick-on craft eyes

1 Fold the sheet from corner to corner, then in half again.

2 Open out the last fold.

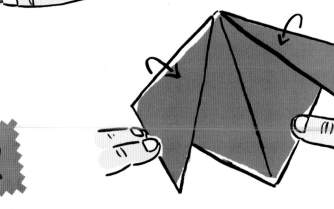

3 Fold down the two corners to make the ears.

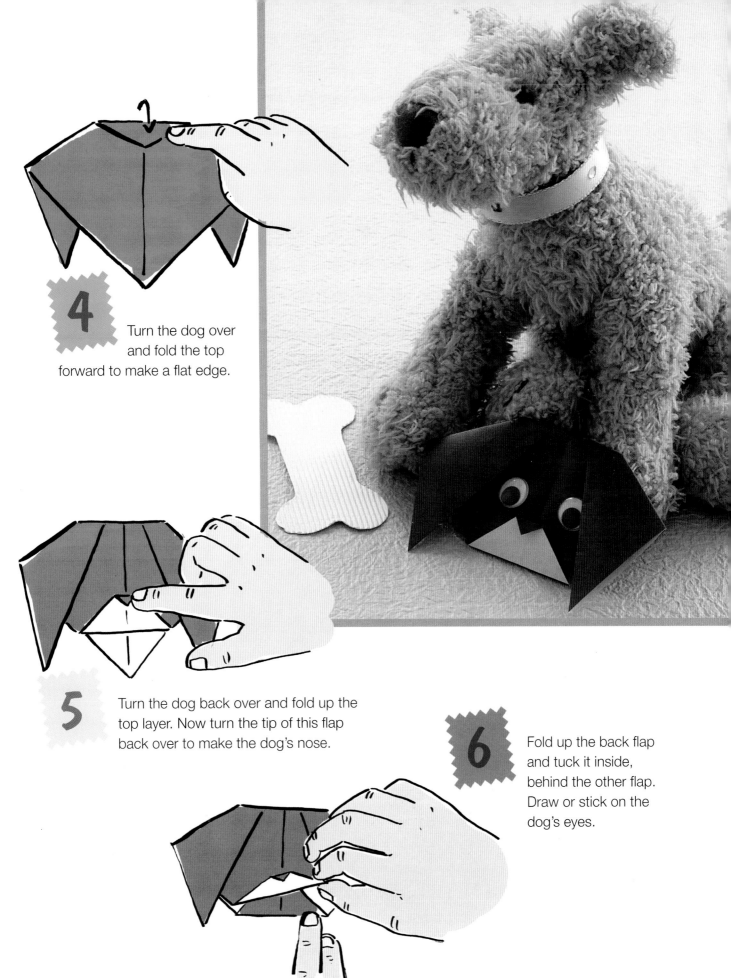

4 Turn the dog over and fold the top forward to make a flat edge.

5 Turn the dog back over and fold up the top layer. Now turn the tip of this flap back over to make the dog's nose.

6 Fold up the back flap and tuck it inside, behind the other flap. Draw or stick on the dog's eyes.

neko (origami cat)

Make origami cats as friends for your origami dogs (see page 18). Each cat will become a real character as soon as you draw on eyes, a nose, and set of whiskers using a marker pen.

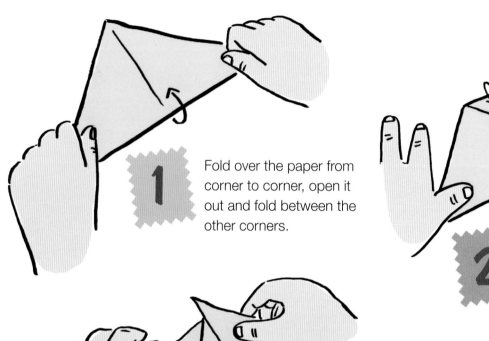

1 Fold over the paper from corner to corner, open it out and fold between the other corners.

2 Turn back the top of the triangle, making a fold about ¾ in. (2 cm) from the tip.

3 Fold up the right-hand corner from the center crease at an angle so that it just covers the triangle made in the previous step.

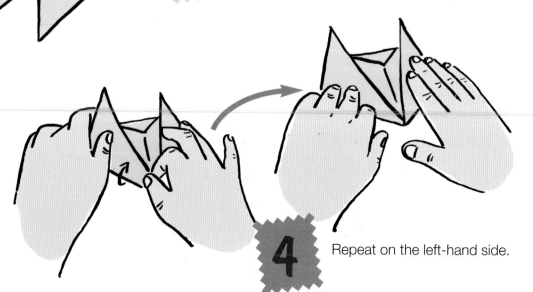

4 Repeat on the left-hand side.

5 Turn the paper over and draw the cat's eyes, nose, and whiskers onto her face.

tissue-paper flowers

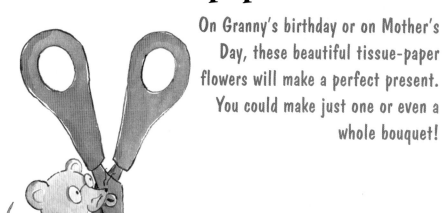

On Granny's birthday or on Mother's Day, these beautiful tissue-paper flowers will make a perfect present. You could make just one or even a whole bouquet!

You will need:

☆☆☆☆☆☆☆☆☆☆☆

Tissue paper in different colors

Ruler

Scissors

Pipe cleaners

A straight twig about 12 in. (30 cm) long for each flower you make

1 Measure and cut 10 pieces of tissue paper 9 ½ x 12-in. (24 x 30-cm). Lay them on top of each other, mixing up the colors.

2 Fold all the layers of tissue paper over together by about 1¼ in. (3 cm) and make a crease.

3 Turn the pile of tissue over and fold the layers over by the same amount again. Keep turning and folding until you have made a zigzag "fan" of folded tissue paper.

4 Take a large pipe cleaner and twist it tightly around the middle of the tissue paper. Cut both ends into a curved petal shape.

5 Carefully pull each layer of paper out to form the petals.

6 Twist the pipe cleaner onto the end of a twig. You could add a paper leaf shape for a finishing touch.

tissue-paper flowers 23

Chapter 2

Natural materials

walnut babies

You'll go nuts over these sweet little walnut babies and their mother. Halves of walnut shells have been turned into perfect cradles for the babies, which are made from wooden beads, decorated with bits of ribbon and fabric. Make the mother by adding an apron and headscarf to an upright whole nut.

1 Ask an adult for some help breaking some walnuts in two, then remove the nuts from inside. Take a small piece of cotton wool and roll it into a ball shape. Spread a little glue inside the walnut half and push the cotton wool inside.

You will need:
☆☆☆☆☆☆☆☆☆☆☆☆

Whole walnuts

Cotton wool

PVA glue

Scraps of fabric

Scissors

Rickrack braid

Ribbon

Wooden beads

Felt-tipped pens

2 Lay another walnut half flat side down onto the fabric and draw around it with a pen. Cut out the oval shape with a pair of scissors.

Make your own **WALNUT FAMILY** to play with!

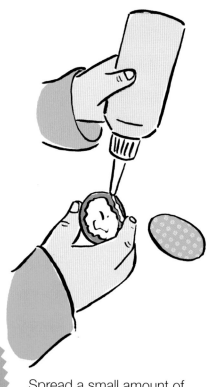

3 Spread a small amount of glue around the edge of the nutshell and stick the fabric in place over the cotton wool.

4 Glue a short length of rickrack braid round the edge of the nutshell, starting and finishing at one end of the shell.

5 To make the baby's head, tie a piece of ribbon around a bead, using a little dab of glue to hold it in place. Tie into a bow and trim the ends short.

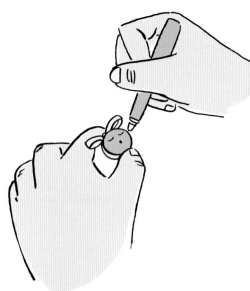

6 Draw a face on the bead with colored felt-tipped pens, marking semicircles for the closed eyes of sleeping babies and dots for the open eyes of awake babies.

7 Fix the head onto the nutshell with a spot of glue, hiding the join in the rickrack.

8 To make a walnut mother, use a whole walnut. Cut a small apron from fabric and glue it onto the nut with a short length of ribbon. Cut a small triangle of fabric and glue it onto the bead to make a headscarf, then glue the bead onto the walnut. Then tie a short piece of ribbon into a bow and glue it onto the walnut, just below the "head".

dried-flower fairies

Pressing flowers is a craft that dates back to the nineteenth century and is still popular today. Pick colorful flowers and leaves (make sure that you have permission first) and then put them in a flower press or between the pages of a heavy book for about a week. When the blooms have dried out and are nice and flat, use them to create all sorts of pictures, like these pretty flower fairies, which can be made into cards or put in frames to give as gifts.

You will need:

☆☆☆☆☆☆☆☆☆☆☆☆

Fresh flowers and leaves

A flower press or a few heavy books (telephone directories or heavy catalogs are good for this)

Fairy template (page 127)

White and colored paper

Cream and colored card

A pencil and ruler

Scissors

A glue stick

1 Collect colorful fresh flowers and small leaves. Find a place in your room where you can leave a pile of books that won't be moved for a week! Find a few large, heavy books that are all about the same size and won't be needed for a week. (If you have your own flower press, you won't need the books.)

2 Open one book and lay a piece of white paper over one of the pages. Arrange the flowers on the paper so they don't touch or overlap. Lay another piece of paper on top of the flowers and close the book.

3 Pile a few more books on top for extra weight. Leave for about a week.

4 Using the fairy template on page 127, cut out a fairy shape, then draw round it on plain colored paper and cut it out.

5 Stick it on to a piece of cream card about 6 in. (15 cm) by 4 in. (10 cm), adding a piece of paper for the fairy's hair.

6 Lift off the books, open the paper, and carefully remove the flowers. Arrange them on the paper fairy to make a pretty dress and hat. When you are happy with the arrangement, carefully lift each flower or petal and dab some glue onto the paper. Press the petal or flower down gently to stick it in place.

7 Cut a 7 x 5-in. (17.5 x 12.5-cm) piece of colored card and fold it in half. Glue the flower fairy onto the front, leaving an even border of colored card all the way around.

natural inks

When September comes and the hedgerows are full of fruit, it's fun to go picking blackberries and raspberries. You'll want to eat most of what you pick, but why not try making these natural inks with some of your harvest? Alternatively, if you are out in the country, just squash some berries with a stone, find a feather to write with, and leave messages for the fairies.

Remember—many berries are poisonous, so only use ones that an adult tells you are safe.

You will need:

Raspberries or blackberries

A sieve

A bowl

A spoon

Salt

White vinegar

Little jars

A feather

1 Put about half a cup of berries in a sieve over a bowl. Squash the berries with the back of a spoon. The juice will drip into the bowl underneath.

2 Add ½ tablespoon of salt to the juice. This will stop it going bad.

WRITE NOTES to your FRIENDS with natural ink!

3 Add ½ tablespoon of vinegar to the mixture. This will stop the color from fading too quickly. Mix well and pour your ink into a small jar.

4 Dip a feather into the ink and start writing. You will need to dip into the ink after every two or three letters.

Question

What color ink does lemon juice make?

Answer

Invisible!

To make invisible ink, simply squeeze a lemon and write with the juice, using the feather or a paintbrush. To reveal the secret message, mix a tablespoon of baking soda with a tablespoon of water and brush the mixture over the paper (grape juice will also work well). Keep this information away from your enemies!

eggshell mosaic mirror

The earliest mosaics were made by the Romans thousands of years ago. They used tiny square of pottery called tesserae to make beautiful pictures. Try making your own mosaic using eggshells colored with food dyes and broken into small pieces. Decorate a mirror frame or make your own picture or pattern on a piece of stiff card.

You will need:

★★★★★★★★★★★

Eggshells

Bowls

Water

Food coloring

Paper towel

A mirror in a wide frame or a rectangle of strong card

Paint and a brush

PVA glue

1 Wash the eggshells thoroughly. Pour water into the bowls and put a few drops of food coloring in each. The more food coloring that you use, the stronger the color of the finished eggshells will be. Put the eggshells into the colored water.

2 Leave the eggshells in the colored water for at least 1 hour. Take them out and if you would like a stronger color, pop them back into the water for a while. When you are happy with the colors, remove the eggshells and rinse them under the tap. Leave them to dry on paper towel.

Create a beautiful MOSAIC with pieces of COLORED eggshell.

3

Break up the colored
eggshells into smallish
pieces. Put the different
colors into separate bowls.

4 Paint the mirror
frame, taking care
not to get paint on
the mirror. If you do, clean it off
with a damp cloth. Leave the
frame to dry and then paint a
second coat if the first is
streaky.

5

Spread PVA
glue onto the frame
and stick the small pieces of
eggshell onto it. You can make up any
pattern you like. You can either cover the whole frame with
eggshells, so that there are no gaps, or design a more spread-out
pattern like the one in the photo. Leave the glue to dry.

apple-print t-shirts

Apple printing is super easy—just cut the apple in half and print away! You can use potatoes, too, by just cutting a shape from them that you want to print. Make sure that you use fabric paints for T-shirts or other clothes that will need to be washed. For paper you can use PVA paints.

Remember to ask an adult to help you with the cutting.

You will need:

☆☆☆☆☆☆☆☆☆☆☆☆

Apples

A sharp knife

Paper towel

Fabric paints

Paper plates

Plain T-shirts

A potato

1 First, ask an adult to cut an apple in half. Remove the stalk and dry the surface with paper towel. Put some fabric paint onto a plate and dip the cut apple into it. Press it lightly onto a scrap of paper to try out the print and to remove any excess paint.

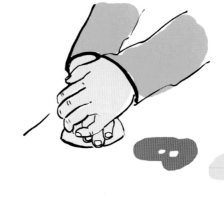

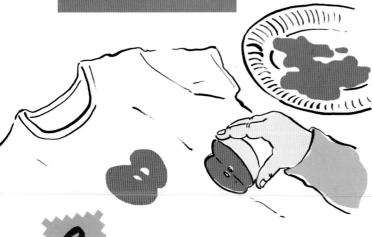

2 Press the apple firmly onto the T-shirt. Carefully remove the apple. Dab off any remaining paint with a paper towel.

3 Dip the apple into a different color paint and print an apple shape on either side of the first print.

Tip

You can use potato prints to make all sorts of different designs. If you want to make perfect shapes when you're printing, using a cookie cutter is a good way of doing it. Ask an adult to cut a potato in half with a sharp knife, then push a cookie cutter into the cut side. Use a rounded knife to cut the potato from around the cutter. Remove the cutter to leave the shape, ready for printing.

4 Get an adult to cut one of the potatoes in half. On one half cut a leaf shape and on the other a small stalk shape. (You may need to ask an adult to help with this.) Print a green leaf onto the middle apple. Mix a little red and green paint together to make brown. Use this to print a stalk onto each apple. Leave to dry and then follow the instructions on the fabric paint to fix the prints so that they don't wash off.

apple-print t-shirts 37

pumpkin animals

Try something different for Halloween this year. Instead of carving a pumpkin, make vegetable monsters with your pumpkins and squash. You can make all sorts of funny faces and bodies and, when you have finished playing, you can cook and eat them for supper! Yummy!

You will need:

☆☆☆☆☆☆☆☆☆☆☆☆

Pumpkins and squash in any shape, size, and color

A selection of other vegetables—carrots, sprouts, eggplant (aubergines), and zucchini (courgettes) are all great

Pumpkin seeds, sunflower seeds, fresh ginger, bay leaves

Cocktail sticks

Wooden skewers

1 Lay all your vegetables out on the table so that you can see what you have got. Play around with different arrangements to create some crazy creatures!

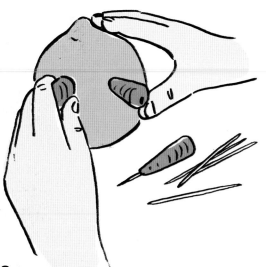

2 Slices of vegetables can become eyes or ears when held in place with cocktail sticks. Push one end of a cocktail stick into the vegetable that you would like to use and then push the other end into your pumpkin.

38

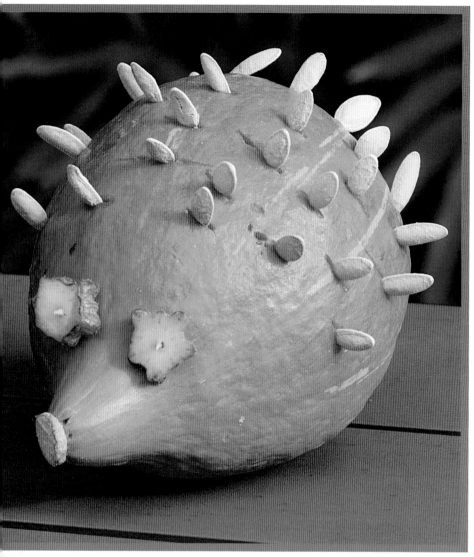

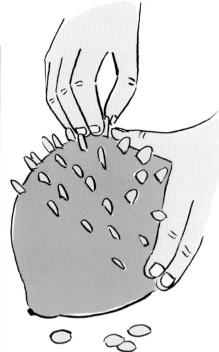

3 Seeds make great spikes for hedgehogs. Push them into a squash, using the pointed top of the squash as a nose. You can also push seeds into pumpkins to give them eyebrows, teeth, noses, and ears.

4 Join two squash together using a wooden skewer. Push one half of the skewer into one squash and the other half into another squash. Ask an adult to help if the skin of the squash is very tough.

6

Bay leaves are a good shape to use as hair, headdresses, and decoration on your creatures. It is easy to push cocktail sticks through them, and these can then be pushed into the pumpkins.

5 Make horns, ears, arms, and eyes by attaching vegetables to the squash with cocktail sticks.

Chapter 3

Simple sewing

spoon puppets

Spoon puppets are quick and easy to make. Draw faces onto wooden spoons or spatulas and sew clothes using simple running stitch and scraps of fabric. Pinking shears give a pretty zigzag edge to the fabric, but don't worry if you haven't got any—your puppet won't mind! Make different characters and act out your favorite stories for friends and family.

You will need:

☆☆☆☆☆☆☆☆☆☆☆

A wooden spoon or spatula

Felt-tipped pens

Scraps of fabric (recycle worn-out clothes)

Pinking shears (if you have some)

Scissors

Yarn (wool) and needle with a large eye

Scraps of yarn (wool)

PVA glue

Ribbons and buttons for decoration

1 Draw a face onto the back of the wooden spoon or spatula using felt-tipped pens.

2 Cut out a piece of fabric measuring about 12 x 5 in. (30 x 13 cm)—if you have pinking shears, use them to give a zigzag edge. Cut a length of yarn and thread the large needle. Sew running stitch (see page 119) across the top of the fabric, leaving about 4 in. (10 cm) of yarn at each end.

Why not PUT ON A PLAY with your spoon puppets?

3

Gather up the fabric by pulling the yarn (see page 121), then tie it around the spoon, fastening with a knot or a bow.

4

Cut the yarn scraps into lengths to make your puppet's hair. Dab some glue on the top of the spoon and stick the yarn in place. Leave it to dry.

5

You can decorate your puppet in a number of ways depending on its character. Tie ribbon in its hair; glue or tie ribbon around its neck; or make buttons from felt and sew them onto the fabric. You could also cut out a tie shape in fabric and glue it in place.

ladybug pincushion

Everyone should have one of these bright, practical ladybug pincushions in their sewing kit. Why not give them as presents to family and friends, or stitch several to sell at a school fundraiser?

You will need:

⭐⭐⭐⭐⭐⭐⭐⭐⭐⭐⭐⭐

Ladybug templates (page 123)

Paper and a pencil, to make the pattern pieces

Scissors

Red and black felt

Pins

Red and black embroidery floss (thread)

A needle

Fiberfill (stuffing)

2 shank buttons (with loops underneath instead of holes) for the ladybug's eyes

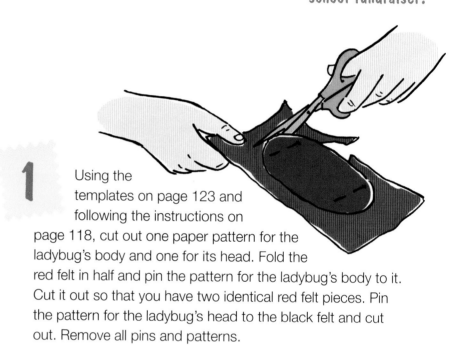

1 Using the templates on page 123 and following the instructions on page 118, cut out one paper pattern for the ladybug's body and one for its head. Fold the red felt in half and pin the pattern for the ladybug's body to it. Cut it out so that you have two identical red felt pieces. Pin the pattern for the ladybug's head to the black felt and cut out. Remove all pins and patterns.

2 Cut a length of black embroidery floss (thread) and tie a knot at one end. Thread the needle. Starting on the underside of the felt and using running stitch (see page 119), sew the ladybug's head onto one of the body pieces. Finish with a knot on the underside of the felt. Trim the floss. Cut out small circles of black felt and sew them onto the ladybug's body in the same way, using black floss.

3 Starting and finishing with a knot on the underside of the felt, sew a line of black backstitch (see page 119) down the middle of the ladybug's body. Trim the floss.

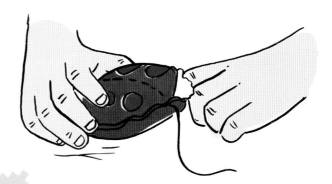

4 Pin the front and back pieces of the ladybug together and, using red floss, stitch around them with running stitch, leaving a small opening. Remove the pins.

5 Push Fiberfill (stuffing) through the opening to stuff the ladybug (see page 120). Use plenty of Fiberfill so that the pincushion will be nice and plump. Sew up the opening and finish with a knot on the underside.

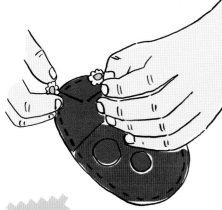

6 Sew the shank buttons onto the ladybug's head (see page 121) so that they look like eyes.

yo-yo necklace

You will need:

☆☆☆☆☆☆☆☆☆☆

A pen

An old CD

A coffee mug

Scraps of thin fabric in different colors

A needle and thread

5 big buttons

Ribbon

This pretty necklace is simply made from scraps of colorful fabric—maybe even from old clothes that have worn out. You will need to raid your family button box to find some large colorful buttons for the perfect finish. And you needn't just make a necklace. Try making a bracelet using rows of small yo-yos or sew a safety pin on the back of a bigger yo-yo to make a brooch.

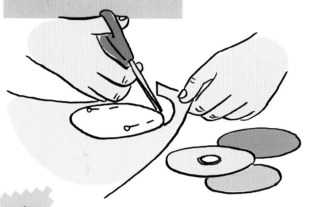

1 Use the CD to draw around. Draw three circles on different fabrics and cut them out. Now use the top of the coffee mug to draw around. Draw two smaller circles and cut them out.

2 Thread the needle with a length of thread. Sew a few small stitches over and over at the edge of one of the fabric circles, so that the thread is firmly attached. Now sew running stitch all the way round the circle (see page 119).

3 At the end, carefully pull the thread to gather up the fabric, making the yo-yo. Finish with a few small stitches over and over in the same place, so it doesn't come undone. Cut the thread and flatten the yo-yo. In the same way make yo-yos with each of the other circles.

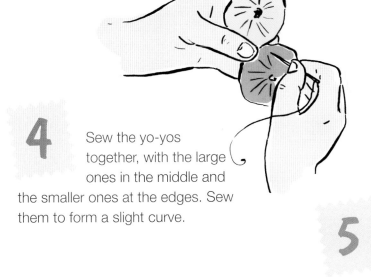

4 Sew the yo-yos together, with the large ones in the middle and the smaller ones at the edges. Sew them to form a slight curve.

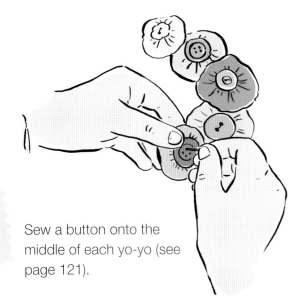

5 Sew a button onto the middle of each yo-yo (see page 121).

6 Cut two lengths of ribbon about 8 in. (20 cm) long. Sew a few small stitches through the edge of an outer (small) yo-yo, then stitch one end of a ribbon to it. Secure the ribbon in place with some more stitches, then trim the thread. Repeat with the second length of ribbon, sewing it to the yo-yo on the other side.

TIE the necklace around your neck WITH A BOW!

Make this necklace with BUTTONS and RIBBON!

button necklace

White buttons are always the most boring buttons in the button box, but they don't need to be. Here's how to use them to make a really attractive, modern-looking necklace— a great present for your big sister, or maybe you will want to keep it for yourself. But you needn't keep to white buttons. Use the same method to make bright, colorful necklaces by using an assortment of different colored buttons from your button box with colorful beads in between. Using four-hole buttons gives an interesting off-center effect, but two-hole buttons work too.

You will need:

2 yards (2 metres) narrow pink silk ribbon (⅜ in./1 cm or narrower)

2 yards (2 metres) narrow white silk ribbon (⅜ in./1 cm or narrower)

2 needles with wide eyes

26 matt white round glass beads, ⅜ in. (1 cm) in diameter

25 white buttons with four holes, ¾ in. (2 cm) in diameter

Scissors

PVA glue

1 Thread one needle with the pink ribbon and the other needle with the white ribbon. Take a bead and thread it onto the pink ribbon. Now pull the pink ribbon tightly against the side of the bead hole while you pass the needle with the white ribbon through the same bead. Pull the bead along the ribbons until it is about 12 in. (30 cm) from the ends. Pull the ends of the ribbons so they are even and tie them together in a knot to stop the bead coming off.

2 Now add a button next to the bead. First, pass the pink ribbon over the top of the button and down through a hole. Next pass the white ribbon under the button and up through the same hole. Bring the two ribbons together, white on top and pink beneath, and pass the two ends through another glass bead.

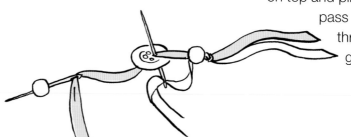

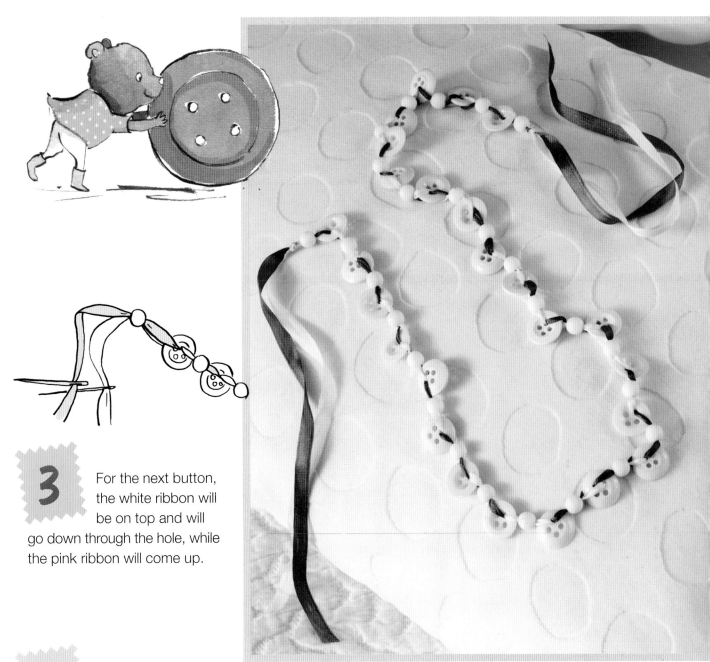

3 For the next button, the white ribbon will be on top and will go down through the hole, while the pink ribbon will come up.

4 Continue threading in the same way until all 25 buttons and 26 glass beads are in place. You should finish with a glass bead.

5 After the last bead, tie the two ribbons into a knot, leaving tails long enough (about 12 in./30 cm) to tie into a fastening bow. Cut off any extra ribbon. Add a smear of PVA glue to all four ribbon ends to seal the threads. When the glue is dry, cut the ribbon ends neatly on a slant.

teddy bear

This little teddy bear can be made from any type of fabric. Have you got a favorite dress or t-shirt that is too worn out to pass on to someone else? Make a teddy bear out of it to keep as a special friend.

You will need:

Teddy template (page 124)

Paper and a pencil for making a pattern

Two 12-in. (30-cm) square pieces of fabric

Pins

Small buttons

Fiberfill (stuffing)

A sewing needle and matching thread

3-in. (7.5-cm) length of string or yarn

A tapestry needle

1 Using the teddy-bear template on page 124 and following the instructions on page 118, cut out a paper pattern. Place your two fabric squares one on top of the other, pin the pattern on top, and cut out your teddy-bear shapes.

2 Sew small buttons on the front piece of the teddy bear. You might also want to give him some button eyes.

3 Wrong sides together, pin the front to the back of the teddy. Starting at the head, sew the two sides together using tiny backstitches (see page 119). Sew about ¼ in. (6 mm) in from the edge. Leave a gap of about 1 in. (2.5 cm) at the top so you can stuff the teddy.

4

Stuff the teddy bear, using the blunt end of a pencil to push the fiberfill down into the legs and arms (see page 120). Sew up the gap.

5

To hang up the teddy bear, thread the string or yarn onto the tapestry needle, push it through the top of the teddy, and tie a knot.

Make your own TEDDY bear to CUDDLE!

chicken egg cozy

This chicken egg cozy will keep your egg lovely and warm until you are ready to eat it. Decorate it with embroidery stitches in contrasting colors to show off your sewing skills.

You will need:

Chicken head and comb templates (page 124)

Paper and a pencil for making patterns

Scissors

Scraps of colored felt

A small coin

Scraps of yarn (wool) or embroidery floss (thread)

A tapestry needle

2 buttons

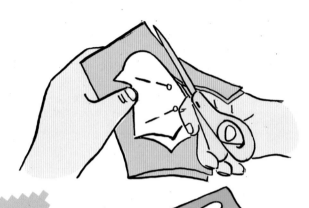

1 Using the templates on page 124 and following the instructions on page 118, cut out one paper pattern for the chicken head and one for its comb. Fold one piece of felt in half and pin onto it the pattern for the head. Cut it out so that you have two chicken heads. Choose a different color of felt for the comb and pin the pattern onto it. Cut out one comb.

2 Find a coin that is bigger than your button. Choose a third color of felt, draw around the coin twice onto the felt, and cut out two circles for the eyes.

3 Thread the tapestry needle with a contrasting color of yarn (wool) or embroidery floss (thread), sew one eye circle onto each of the chicken head pieces. (Check that the eyes will both be on the outside of the chicken head when you sew the two sides together.) Tie a knot in the end of the thread. Then, from the outside, push the needle down through the center of the eye circle and pull it back up on the outside of the eye, then down through the middle again and keep going like this. Sew about 6 stitches to make a pattern like the rays of the sun. Stitch the buttons in place on top of the circles (see page 121).

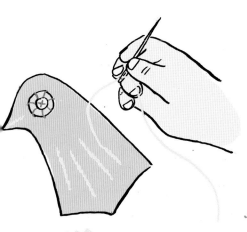

4 Sew patterns on the chicken's beak and neck using stem stitch (see page 120).

5 Pin the two head pieces together with the comb in place in between them. Starting at the bottom, use blanket stitch (see page 120) to stitch the two sides together. When you reach the comb, use a simple running stitch to stitch through all three layers, then change back to blanket stitch for the rest of the chicken.

6 If you wish, you can add more decoration by stitching in blanket stitch around the comb and both sides of the bottom of the egg cozy—but remember, you need a space for your egg, so don't sew the two sides of the base together!

Use your NICE NEW EGG COZY when you have eggs for dinner!

Chapter 4

Creative costumes

alien head

Do you need an alien costume that is out of this world? This super-scary papier-mâché head will top off any weird and wonderful costume you can put together from your dressing-up box.

Remember: if you are planning to make the head for a party or for Halloween, you will need to start work the week before to give it time to dry.

You will need:

A balloon that is bigger than your head

Newspaper

PVA glue and water

A bowl and spoon

Scissors

Cardboard

Green and white paints

A paint brush

3 polystyrene balls

3 pipe cleaners

A scrap of black felt

Sticky tape

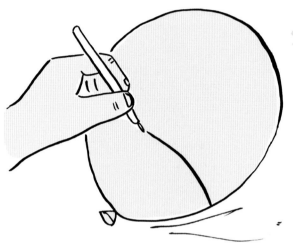

1 Blow up the balloon until it is bigger than your head, knot it, and draw a line around it to mark the bottom edge of the alien head.

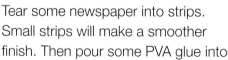

2 Tear some newspaper into strips. Small strips will make a smoother finish. Then pour some PVA glue into a bowl. Add a little water and stir. Keep adding a little water at a time until the glue is like runny paint. Dip the newspaper strips into the glue and paste them onto the balloon down to the pen line. Cover the balloon completely and keep adding paper until is about four layers thick. Leave it to dry in a warm place. This may take several days.

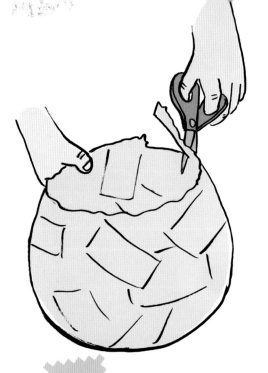

4

You may need to ask an adult with a craft knife to help you with this part. Draw a large mouth shape for your face in the front of the head and cut it out. Now paint the whole head green. If the paint is patchy, let it dry and then paint another coat.

3 When the newspaper is dry and hard, pop the balloon and remove the bits from inside the head. Trim round the edge with scissors to make it smooth. Make sure your head will fit inside!

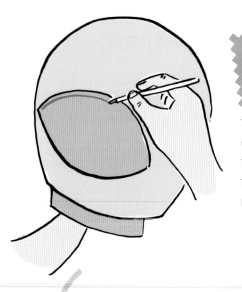

5 Hold a piece of cardboard inside the head and draw onto it the shape of the top of the mouth. Now draw on some ferocious, jagged teeth. Cut them out, making sure that you leave a strip of cardboard above the teeth so that you can stick them to the head. Do the same for the bottom of the mouth. Paint the teeth white. When they are dry, glue them inside the mouth, holding them in place until they are stuck.

6 Push a polystyrene ball onto the end of each pipe cleaner, using a small dab of glue to hold it in place. Glue a small black circle of felt onto each one to make it into an eyeball.

7 Cut three small slits in the top of the head (ask an adult to help you do this with a craft knife) and push the ends of the pipe cleaners through them. Tape the ends of the pipe cleaners to the inside of the head to hold them firmly in place.

Now put the head on to become a SUPER-SCARY ALIEN!

fairy wings

Transform yourself into a beautiful butterfly or a fluttering fairy with these pretty, easy-to-sew wings. Decorate them with lots of small bows or leave them plain so that they are even quicker to make.

You will need:

☆☆☆☆☆☆☆☆☆☆☆

Pink net, measuring 59 in. (150 cm) long by the standard fabric width

A marker pen

Pins

Scissors

Wide pink ribbon measuring 100 in. (260 cm)

Embroidery floss (thread) and needle

Pieces of narrow ribbon for the decorating bows

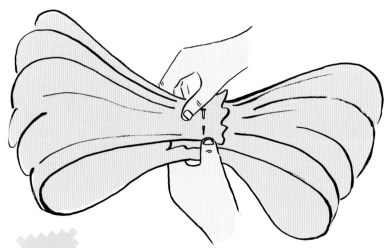

1 The first stage is a bit tricky to do on your own, so you may need to ask someone to help you. Lay out the net on the table or floor. Find the middle of the net by folding it in half and mark the halfway point with a marker pen. Unfold it again. Now gather the net up into a long sausage shape and fold the two ends into the middle, overlapping them slightly. Keeping the net gathered up, pin the ends to hold them in place.

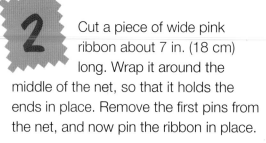

2 Cut a piece of wide pink ribbon about 7 in. (18 cm) long. Wrap it around the middle of the net, so that it holds the ends in place. Remove the first pins from the net, and now pin the ribbon in place.

Become a **DAINTY LITTLE FAIRY** for the day!

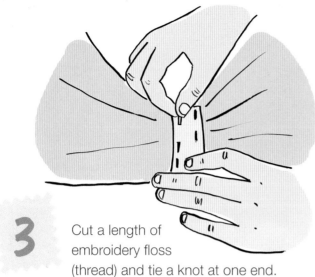

3 Cut a length of embroidery floss (thread) and tie a knot at one end. Thread the needle. Stitch through all the layers of net and ribbon so that the ribbon is firmly held in place. Finish with a few small stitches to secure the floss. Trim the floss and remove the pins.

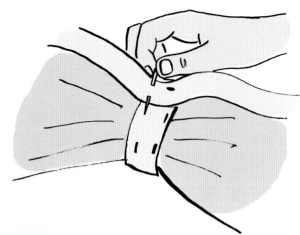

4 Now sew on the rest of the wide, pink ribbon; this will tie the wings to your back. Find the middle of the ribbon by folding it. Starting with a knot in the floss, sew the middle of the long ribbon across the piece of ribbon that is fixed around the net. Stitch it firmly, finishing with a few small stitches to secure the floss. Trim the floss.

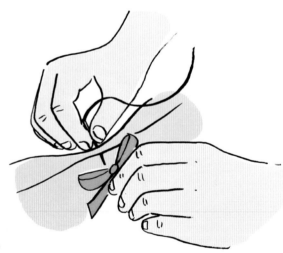

5 If you want to decorate your wings with little bows, cut the narrow ribbon into lengths about 12 in. (30 cm) long. Tie them into bows. Tie a knot at one end of the embroidery floss and, working from the underside, sew each bow onto the wings, stitching through the net and the ribbon a few times and finishing with a few small stitches on the underside. Trim the floss.

6

To wear the wings, ask someone to hold them against your back for you. Pull the ends of the wide pink ribbon over your shoulders and cross them over your chest. Wrap them around your back and then bring them around to your front. Tie them in a pretty bow.

Papier-mâché masks

In the same way as you can make an alien head (see page 58) with a balloon and papier mâché, you can also make these cute animal masks. Scary masks would be just as easy. In fact, you can use this papier-mâché base for any sort of mask.

Remember: if you are planning to make a mask for a party or play, you will need to start work the week before to give it time to dry.

1 Blow up the balloon to the same size as your head and tie a knot.

You will need:

☆☆☆☆☆☆☆☆☆☆☆☆

A balloon about the same size as your head

Newspaper

PVA glue

Water

A bowl and spoon

Scissors

Felt-tipped pens

White paint and brush

Templates (page 122)

Felt

2 Tear some newspaper into strips. Small strips will make a smoother finish.

3 Pour some PVA glue into a bowl. Add a little water and stir. Keep adding a little water at a time until the glue is like runny paint. Dip pieces of newspaper into the glue and start to paste them over one half of the balloon. Keep pasting on pieces until half of the balloon is covered with at least four layers of paper.

4 Leave in a warm place until the newspaper is hard and dry. This may take several days.

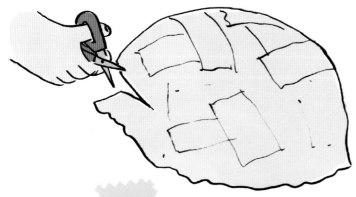

5 Burst the balloon! Remove it and trim round the mask with scissors to neaten the edges.

6 Draw two eyes on the mask and cut them out. You may need an adult to help you draw them in the right place and to cut them out.

7 Paint the front of the mask and leave it to dry. It might need two coats. Let the first coat dry before you paint again.

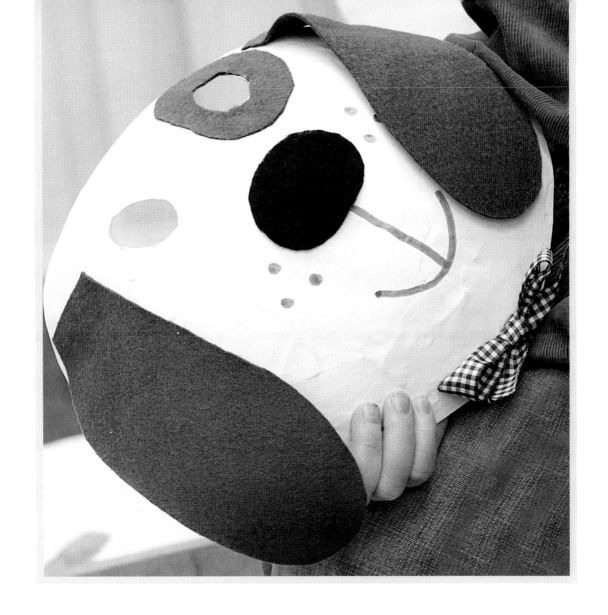

8 Using the templates on page 122 and following the instructions on page 118, cut out the ears, nose, and other decorations for your mask from the felt. Glue them onto the mask with PVA glue and leave to dry.

Pretend you're a GRIZZLY BEAR with this great hat!

animal hat

This furry animal hat is so cozy you won't want to take it off. Fur material is available from fabric stores in a range of different animal prints and is fun to use, as it doesn't fray and is easy to cut. Why not make a tail as well? Simply cut a strip of fur fabric and sew it onto a piece of ribbon long enough to tie around your waist.

You will need:

Templates (page 126)

Paper and a pencil to make the pattern pieces

Pins

Scissors

Fake fur

Scraps of felt

A needle and thread

1 Using the templates on page 126 and following the instructions on page 118, cut out a paper pattern for the front of the hat, one for the back, and one for the bear ear. Pin the pattern pieces to the fake fur (you may find it easier to pin them to the back of the fur) and cut them out. You will need four ears. Remove the pins and the patterns and set the front and back pieces aside.

2 Using the template on page 126, cut out a paper pattern for the bear's inner ear. Pin the pattern to the felt and cut out two inner ears. Pin each felt inner ear to the furry side of a fur ear. Cut a length of thread and tie a knot at one end. Thread the needle. Working from the back of the fur ears, sew an inner ear to each of two fur ears with running stitch (see page 119). Finish with a knot on the back and trim the thread. Remove the pins.

3 Now pin each of the other fur ear pieces to the back of these ears, so that the non-furry sides are together and the ear is furry on both sides. Sew them together with running stitch.

Tip

Why not make an animal hat for your younger brother or sister? You could make them a cute tiger hat: follow the project as normal, but use the tiger ear templates on page 126 instead of the bear ones.

4 Lay the back part of the fur hat flat on the table with the furry side up. Position the ears on top of the fur so that the straight edges are overlapping the top edge of the back piece, and pin together. Knot one end of the thread again and, working from the back of the hat, sew the ears in place with a few running stitches. Finish with a knot on the back of the hat and trim the thread. Remove the pins.

5 Lay the front of the hat onto the back, furry sides together. Pin the layers together, leaving the flat edge open. Sew them together using running stitch, starting and ending with a few small stitches to hold the thread in place. Turn the hat the right way out and put it on your head.

AVAST, me hearties! Turn yourself into a PIRATE!

pirate hat & eye patch

Shiver me timbers, it's Captain Jack! Have fun playing pirates with a great hat and eye patch that make an easy sewing project. Cut a square of spotty fabric and fold it in half to make a necktie to complete your costume.

You will need:

Templates (page 123)

Paper and a pencil, to make the pattern pieces

Pins

Scissors

Black felt

White felt

White embroidery floss (thread) and needle

2 black buttons

Black thread and needle

Black elastic

1

Using the templates on page 123 and following the instructions on page 118, cut out a paper pattern for the front and the back of the hat. Pin these to the black felt and cut out one of each. Remove the pins and patterns.

2

Using the templates on page 123, cut out paper patterns for one skull and two bones. Pin these to the white felt and cut out. Remove pins and patterns.

3

Pin the felt skull to the front piece of the hat near the top and in the middle, and one of the bones diagonally beneath it. Sew them in place with white embroidery floss (thread) using running stitch (see page 119), starting and finishing with a few small stitches on the inside of the hat. Remove the pins. Pin the second bone diagonally over the top of the first to make a cross and sew it onto the hat in the same way. Remove the pins.

4

Sew on two buttons for the eye sockets with black thread (see page 121).

5

Pin the two felt pieces together. Cut a length of white embroidery floss (thread) and tie a knot at one end. Thread the needle. Starting from the inside of the hat, use running stitch (see page 119) around the sides and top, leaving the bottom open. Finish with a few small stitches on the inside, and trim the floss. Remove the pins.

6

Using the template on page 123, cut out a paper pattern for the eye patch. Fold the black felt and pin the pattern to it. Cut it out. You will have two eye-patch shapes. Remove the pins and pattern. Cut a length of black thread and tie a knot at one end. Using small stitches, sew one end of the elastic to the top corner of one of the felt pieces, finishing with a few small finishing stitches on the same side as the first knot. Check the elastic will fit around your head, then sew the other end to the opposite top corner of the felt. Make sure the elastic is stitched securely in place.

7

Pin the second felt eye-patch piece to the back of the first, hiding the elastic knots. Cut a length of white embroidery floss and tie a knot at one end. Thread the needle. Working from the back, use running stitch around the edges to join the felt pieces together. Finish with a few small stitches on the back of the patch and trim the floss. Remove the pins.

Put on your hat and eye patch and SAIL THE SEVEN SEAS!

royal crowns

The perfect prop for a school play—loyal subjects will bow down when they see you wearing this majestic crown.

1 Using the template on page 126 and following the instructions on page 118, cut out the template for the royal crown. This gives you one section of the crown. Draw round it onto a piece of scrap cardboard to make a strong template. Using the back (white side) of the gold posterboard, draw around your cardboard template ten times along the bottom edge, making sure that each section joins onto the one before.

2 Cut out the crown. Bend it into a circle, overlapping the ends slightly. Fix it together with paperclips and check that it fits. Glue the overlapping ends together and replace the paper clips to hold it while it dries.

Greetings, YOUR MAJESTY!

3 Cut a 22 x 1¼-in. (56 x 3.5-cm) strip of fake fur. Spread glue around the bottom of the crown and glue the strip of fur in place, making sure that it is well stuck.

4 Glue two 22-in (56-cm) lengths of rickrack around the crown, overlapping the ends slightly at the back. Glue fake jewels at intervals between the two rows of rickrack all the way around the crown.

Chapter 5

Baking and sugarcraft

sugar mice

Too cute to eat but too sweet not to!
What will you do with your sugar mice?

You will need:

Cornstarch (cornflour)

1 pound (450 g) white fondant icing (available from grocery stores or via the Internet)

Food coloring (pink or yellow for body)

Black writing icing

A cup of warm water

1 Put on an apron and wash your hands well with soap and warm water. Dust your work surface with a little cornstarch.

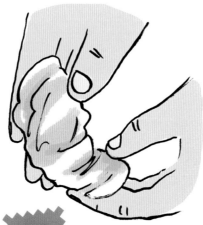

2 For a colored mouse, break off a piece of white fondant icing and add a few drops of food coloring. Spread the color through the icing by folding it and kneading. Keep doing this until the icing is soft to handle and colored evenly all over.

3 Make a mouse-shaped body.

4 Make two round ears and attach them to the body, using a dab of water to stick them down.

Tip

Store your mice in a cardboard box at room temperature—do not refrigerate. Sugar paste can keep for a long time, but is best eaten within 6 months.

5 Make the nose from a small ball of white icing. Attach it with a dab of water. Make eyes with black writing icing.

6 Finally, make a long, thin sausage for the tail and attach it to the underside of the mouse with another dab of water. Leave the mouse to dry.

Serve these SWEET MICE after dinner!

marshmallow snowmen

These cute chaps are easy and fun to make and look gorgeous on the Christmas table. Why not make one snowman for each person as a place setting, or make a winter wonderland by dusting them all with sugar snow on a serving plate?

You will need:

7 oz. (200 g) large white marshmallows

About 10 toothpicks

Scissors

Black writing icing

Colored licorice strips or fruit leather

Chocolate-coated mint sticks or pretzel sticks

Large chocolate drops

4 oz. (115 g) white mini-marshmallows

Confectioners' (icing) sugar, for dusting (optional)

Makes about 10 snowmen

1 Put on an apron and wash your hands well with soap and warm water. Place the marshmallows on a tray.

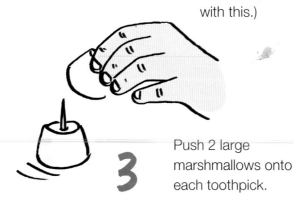

2 Place one large marshmallow on top of another one and measure a toothpick up against them. Using the scissors, cut off the toothpick so that it is a bit shorter than the two marshmallows together. Cut off the other toothpicks to the same length. (You may need help with this.)

3 Push 2 large marshmallows onto each toothpick.

4 Using the writing icing, pipe dots and lines of icing onto the face to make the eyes, nose, and mouth.

5 Cut the licorice strips or fruit leather into thin strips and carefully tie around the snowman's neck for a scarf.

6 To make the arms, break the chocolate-coated mint sticks in half and push into the sides of the large marshmallow.

7 Pipe a small blob of writing icing onto the top of the snowman's head and position a large chocolate drop on top. Pipe another blob of icing in the middle of the chocolate drop and stick a mini-marshmallow on the very top.

8 Finally, using the writing icing again, pipe dots down the front of the snowman to look like buttons.

9 Keep making snowmen like this until you have as many as you want. Arrange them on a tray to serve. To create a fabulous, snowy winter wonderland, dust them all with confectioners' sugar, too.

gingerbread families

Don't just make little people—look for cutters in the shape of a princess, a pony, or a teddy bear. Decorate them with chocolate chips, sweets, or raisins.

You will need:

⭐⭐⭐⭐⭐⭐⭐⭐⭐⭐⭐

2 baking sheets

A sieve

A large mixing bowl

A measuring cup or weighing scales

A measuring jug

A tablespoon

A wooden spoon

A rolling pin

Shaped cookie cutters

Spatula

Ingredients:

2⅓ cups (350 g) self-rising flour

A pinch of salt

1 tablespoon ground ginger

1 cup (200 g) caster sugar

1 stick (115 g) unsalted butter

¼ cup (85 g) light corn syrup (golden syrup)

1 extra-large (large UK) egg

To decorate

Raisins

Edible silver balls (optional)

Sweets

Makes 14 figures, 5 in. (12 cm) long

1 Put on an apron and wash your hands well with soap and warm water.

2 Ask an adult to help you preheat the oven to 325°F (160°C/Gas Mark 3). Get your baking sheet ready by putting some butter on a paper towel and rubbing it lightly over the sheet. This is called "greasing." It will stop the gingerbread from sticking to the tray.

3 Set a sieve over a large mixing bowl. Tip the flour, salt, and ground ginger into the sieve and sift into the bowl. Add the sugar and mix in with a wooden spoon. Make a hollow in the center of the mix.

4 Put the butter and syrup into a small saucepan. Ask an adult to help you melt the butter and corn syrup gently over very low heat—warm the pan just enough to melt the ingredients. Don't let the mixture become hot.

5 Carefully pour the melted mixture into the hollow in the flour.

6 Crack the egg into a small bowl and break up with a fork.

7 Pour the egg into the hollow on top of the melted mixture. Mix all the ingredients with a wooden spoon. As soon as the dough starts to come together, put your hands into the bowl and start to push the barely warm dough together. If the dough is too hot to handle, wait for it to cool.

8 Lightly dust your work surface with some flour. As soon as the dough has come together into a ball, and is no longer crumbly, tip it out of the bowl and onto the work surface.

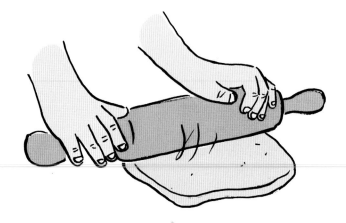

9 With a rolling pin, gently roll out the dough to a large rectangle about ¼ in. (5 mm) thick.

10 Cut out figures with your cutters, then carefully transfer them to the prepared baking sheets with a large spatula. Don't worry if their limbs or heads fall off—just press them back together again. Space the figures well apart, because they will spread in the oven. Gather all the trimmings into a ball, then roll out the dough again and cut more figures as before.

11 Decorate the figures with raisins, silver balls (optional), or sweets.

12 Ask an adult to help you put the baking sheets into the oven. The gingerbread figures will take about 15 minutes to cook. They are ready when they are golden brown. Watch them carefully, because they can quickly burn.

13 Ask an adult to help you remove the trays carefully from the oven and leave them on a heatproof work surface to cool for 5 minutes. This lets the soft cookie mixture become hard. When the figures are firm, gently lift them onto a wire rack, using a large spatula. Let them cool completely. Store in an airtight container and eat within 1 week.

Give your DELICIOUS gingerbread as a PRESENT or eat it yourself!

peppermint creams

Peppermint creams are delicious and easy to make, and they need no cooking. Always let them dry on baking parchment before putting them into boxes.

You will need:

A measuring cup/kitchen scales

A tablespoon

A large bowl

A sieve

A wooden spoon

Baking parchment

A baking tray

A rolling pin

A mini star-shaped cutter or any other small cutter

Ingredients:

1¾ cups (225 g) confectioners' (icing) sugar

4–6 tablespoons sweetened condensed milk

½ teaspoon peppermint extract

Green food coloring (optional)

Makes 20–30 peppermint creams

1 Put on an apron and wash your hands well with soap and warm water. Sift the confectioners' (icing) sugar into a large bowl. Gradually add the condensed milk and peppermint extract, mixing with a wooden spoon. The mixture should come together like dough. It is easier to use your hands towards the end of the mixing.

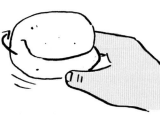

2 Sprinkle some confectioners' sugar onto a clean work surface. Shape the dough into a ball and knead it. To do this put it on the work surface, push it down with your hands and flatten it, fold it over, and turn it around half a turn. Do this again and again for a couple of minutes until your dough is smooth. Sprinkle the surface with more sugar if it sticks.

3 If you like, you can now divide the dough in half and tint one half green using a few drops of the food coloring. Knead the colored dough again until it is green all over without any streaks.

4 Place a sheet of baking parchment onto a tray.

5 On the work surface, roll out the dough to a thickness of ¼ in. (5 mm) using a rolling pin. Stamp out shapes with your cookie cutter and arrange them on the baking parchment. Gather the left-over bits together, knead them again, roll out again, and cut more shapes. Keep doing this till you have used up all your dough.

Let them dry out overnight before packing into PRETTY BOXES.

animal bread rolls

It is exciting to make bread because bread is made with yeast and yeast is alive! As yeast grows, it makes bubbles of carbon dioxide gas in the dough and that's why bread has holes in it. Watch your dough rise and double in size before your eyes as the yeast works its magic. Then make cute animal-shaped rolls—a delicious treat eaten warm with a yummy filling of your choice.

You will need:

☆☆☆☆☆☆☆☆☆☆☆

A baking sheet

Paper towel

A measuring cup or kitchen scales

A large mixing bowl

A measuring jug

A tablespoon

A teaspoon

Kitchen scissors

Plastic wrap (cling film)

A little oil

Ingredients

1⅔ cups (250 g) unbleached all-purpose (plain) flour

1 level teaspoon salt

1 level teaspoon sugar

1 level tablespoon soft butter

1 sachet active dry yeast

⅝ cup (150 ml) warm water (Remember, yeast is alive—hot water will kill it. If the water is too hot for your little finger it is too hot for the yeast.)

Butter, for greasing the baking sheets

A few raisins for eyes

1 Put on an apron and wash your hands well with soap and warm water.

2 Get your baking sheet ready by putting some butter on a paper towel and rubbing it lightly over the sheet. This is called "greasing." It will stop the rolls from sticking to the tray.

3 Put the flour into the mixing bowl. Add the salt and sugar and mix everything together with your hand.

4 Add the butter and rub it into the flour between your fingers and thumb until it is all mixed in and the mixture is crumbly, like bread crumbs.

5 Pour in the yeast and mix it in well.

Making bread rolls is EASY and FUN!

6 Make a hollow in the middle of the flour mixture. Pour the warm water slowly into the hollow so that it makes a pool within the flour.

7 Using your hand, gradually stir the flour into the water—the mixture will turn from a runny mixture to a soft dough as more flour is mixed in. Work the dough with your hand until all the flour has been mixed in. (If there are dry crumbs in the bowl and the dough feels very dry and hard to mix, add a little more water to the bowl, one tablespoon at a time. If the dough is very sticky and sticks to your fingers or the sides of the bowl, add more flour, one tablespoon at a time.)

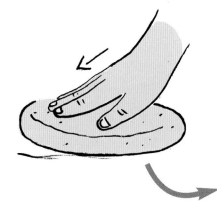
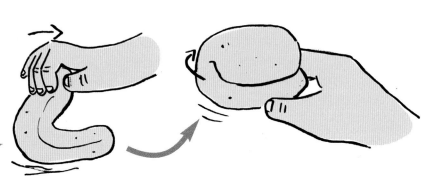

8 Sprinkle a little flour over the work surface and tip the dough out of the bowl onto the surface. Using both hands, knead the dough. To do this, push the ball of dough down and away from you with the heel of your hands, stretching and flattening it as you push. Fold the far edge towards you. Turn the ball around half a turn and stretch the dough out again. Fold and turn again. Keep doing this for about 10 minutes—you'll soon get into a rhythm. It's hard work, but you can take a short rest every now and then. You'll know when the dough is ready because it will begin to feel soft and springy in your hands.

9 Divide the dough into 5 even pieces. Make each piece into an animal shape, using raisins for the eyes. You could make crocodiles, mice, cats, pigs, snakes, or hedgehogs (make the spikes by cutting snips into the dough with kitchen scissors). Place the animal rolls on the baking sheet, spaced well apart.

10 Cut a piece of plastic wrap (cling film) more than big enough to cover the baking sheet. Spread the plastic wrap out on the work surface. Put a few drops of oil onto some kitchen paper and wipe this all over the plastic wrap. Cover your rolls with the plastic wrap, oily side down. Tuck it around the sides. (This will prevent the rolls from drying out.)

11 Leave the tray in a warm place (near a warm stove or above a radiator) for the dough to rise. After about half an hour, your rolls will have doubled in size. (At normal room temperature, this would take 1 to 2 hours.)

12 While the dough is rising, ask an adult to help you turn on the oven to 425°F (220°C/Gas Mark 7).

13 When your animals look nice and plump and the oven is hot, ask an adult to help you place the baking sheets into the oven. Bake until the rolls are golden brown—about 15–20 minutes, depending on the thickness of the rolls. Again with adult help, carefully remove the trays from the oven and tip the rolls onto a wire rack to cool.

Add a SAVORY or SWEET filling or eat the rolls on their own—fresh bread always tastes YUMMY!

Chapter 6

Holiday fun

easter egg card

Make one of these pretty pastel cards for Easter—collect patterned gift wrap to make the egg shape, and decorate with rickrack braid and ribbons in matching colors.

You will need:

Egg template (see page 125)

White paper

A pencil and ruler

Scissors

Thin card in cream and pastel colors

Spotted gift wrap

A glue stick

Chunky rickrack braid

PVA glue

Pastel-colored ribbon

1 Trace the egg template onto the paper and cut it out carefully. Draw around the template onto pastel-colored card and cut the egg out.

2 Cut a 1¼ x 3¾-in. (3 x 9.5-cm) strip of spotted paper. Spread glue on the back and stick it across the egg; trim the ends to the shape of the egg. Cut a 4⅜-in. (11-cm) length of rickrack. Spread PVA glue onto the rickrack and glue it across the egg, turning the ends to the back and gluing them in place.

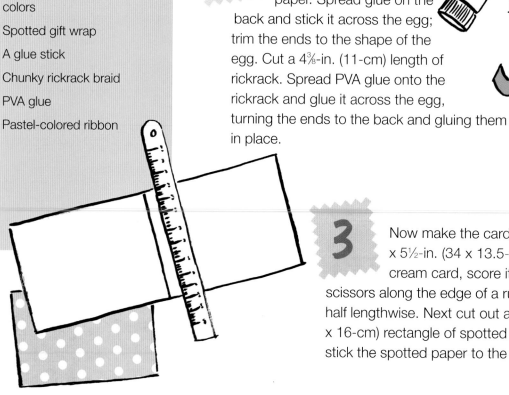

3 Now make the card. Cut out a 13½ x 5½-in. (34 x 13.5-cm) rectangle of cream card, score it by running scissors along the edge of a ruler, and fold it in half lengthwise. Next cut out a 4¾ x 6¼-in. (12 x 16-cm) rectangle of spotted paper. Glue-stick the spotted paper to the front of the card.

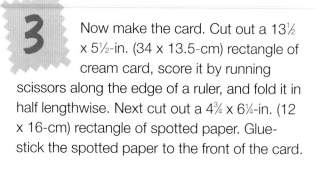

4 Using the glue stick, glue the egg to the center of the card. Cut a 12-in. (30-cm) length of ribbon and tie it in a bow. Glue the bow to the top of the egg with a dab of PVA glue and leave it to dry.

easter basket card

The pretty basket on this card is made by weaving paper. Fill the basket with eggs cut from pastel papers in varying sizes, and add a strip of tissue paper "grass" for a card worthy of any Easter egg hunt.

You will need:

A ruler

A pencil

Thin card in lavender, cream, and pale yellow

Sharp scissors

A glue stick

Scrap paper

Shaped scissors (optional)

Basket, handle, and egg templates (page 125)

Pastel-colored papers for the eggs

Green tissue paper

11-in. (28-cm) length of pink ribbon, 1 in. (2.5 cm) wide

1 Measure and cut out nine strips of yellow card, each ½ x 4⅜ in. (1 x 10.5 cm). Measure and cut out six strips of yellow card, each ¼ x 3½ in. (5 mm x 9 cm).

2 Lay one of the wider strips horizontally on the table. Stick one end of all six thin strips to this with the glue stick so that the strips lie vertically, ⅝ in. (15 mm) apart.

3 Glue the end of a wide strip to the thin strip on the far left, making sure that it butts up to the strip along the top. Weave the rest of the strip through the vertical strips. Glue the other end of this wide strip to the vertical strip on the far right.

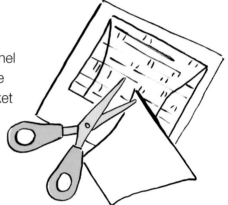

4 Glue another wide strip to the underside of the vertical strip on the far left, butting it up to the previous strip again, and weave as above. Glue the end in place on the far right. Continue until all the thick strips have been woven, remembering to alternate going under and over the strips to form a basket weave. Make sure that all the ends are firmly glued in place.

5 Apply glue stick to the back of the woven panel and stick it onto some scrap paper. Using the basket template on page 125, draw the basket onto the woven panel and cut out.

6 Dab glue onto any ends of the strips that are not stuck down. If you have some shaped scissors, cut out a strip of yellow card about ½ in. (1 cm) wide and long enough to trim the top and bottom of the basket. Glue it in place. Don't worry about this stage if you don't have shaped scissors.

7 Cut out a handle, using the template on page 125. Use your shaped scissors if you have some, otherwise use normal scissors.

8 Cut a 6 x 8½-in. (15.25 x 22-cm) rectangle of cream card.

9 Using the egg templates on page 125, cut out about seven paper eggs in a variety of colors.

10 Glue the basket handle onto the cream card and press down firmly. Arrange the paper eggs on the card and glue them in place.

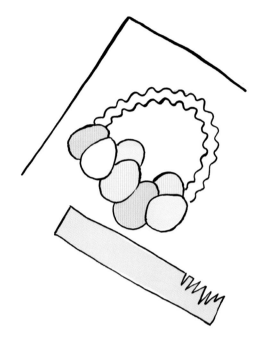

11 Cut a strip of green tissue paper 4⅜ in. (11 cm) long and ¼ in. (2 cm) wide. Make "V"-shaped snips about two-thirds through the width of the tissue paper to look like grass, and stick along the bottom of the eggs.

12 Glue the basket shape in place, making sure that it is well stuck down. Tie a neat bow with the ribbon and stick onto the top of the basket.

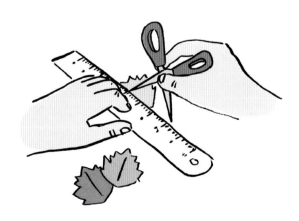

13 Cut a 9 x 12½-in. (23 x 32-cm) rectangle of lavender card. Score down the center, 6¼ in. (16 cm) from each side and fold. Glue the basket card onto this.

Make cards to send to FRIENDS and FAMILY!

cress heads

This is a great project to make at Easter! Give egg heads crazy, cress hairstyles as you grow your own salad. Cress seeds grow quickly and the cress is a delicious in egg sandwiches. To give your egg head funky red hair, use beet seeds instead of cress.

You will need:

Eggs

A pair of scissors with sharp points

Egg cups

A pencil

Acrylic paints

A pointed paintbrush

Potting compost

A teaspoon

Sprouting seeds: cress or beet

Top tip

Don't let the compost dry out, but water sparingly. It is very important that the compost stays fresh, otherwise the seeds may go moldy and fail to germinate.

1 Persuade mom or dad to cook boiled eggs for your breakfast or tea.

2 Ask an adult to slice the tops off neatly with a knife.

3 Eat your egg carefully, making sure that you don't break the shell. Ask the rest of your family to do the same. Carefully wash out the egg shells.

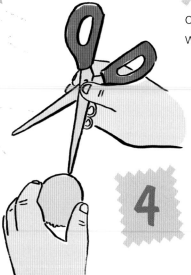

4 Make a small hole at the base of each egg with the point of the scissors (so that water can drain out).

5 Place your eggs in egg cups. Lightly draw faces onto each egg in pencil. Once you are happy with your designs, paint on the faces.

6 Spoon the compost into the shells, stopping just below the top edge. Dampen the compost with a little water.

7 Sprinkle the seeds onto the damp compost. The seeds will germinate (that is, start to grow) in two or three days.

8 When the seedlings are tall enough, give your egg head a hair cut and enjoy an egg sandwich with your home-grown cress.

trick-or-treat basket

Make a cheery trick-or-treat basket to help set the scene for a spooky Halloween. Cover a bucket in colored paper, decorate it with leaf shapes, and hope to fill it with tasty treats when you go out trick or treating. You could make a spookier bucket with witches, cats, and bats instead of leaves.

1 Cut a piece of colored paper long enough to go around the bucket and wide enough to be tucked into it and gathered at the base. Fix the paper in place with clear sticky tape and fold the top of it into the bucket, taping the paper to the inside of the bucket. Make small snips and cut out a section around either side of the handle.

2 Turn the bucket upside down, carefully gather the paper into pleats, and tape it in place. To finish the base neatly, cut a disc of paper slightly smaller than the base and glue it in place over the pleats.

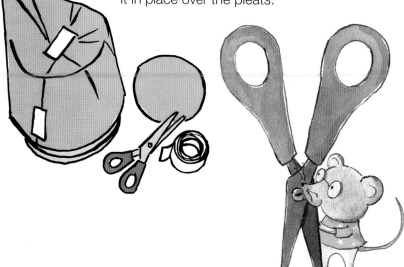

3 Line the bucket with another piece of paper slightly shorter than the bucket. Glue it around the top and hold it in position for a couple of minutes until it sticks firmly.

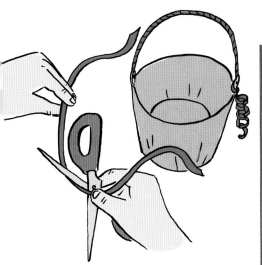

4 Tape the end of the gift ribbon to one side of the handle and wind it around the handle, making sure there are no gaps. Tape the other end in place. Cut a length of ribbon and, holding one blade of a pair of scissors, carefully pull the ribbon over the blade to curl it. Tie the ribbon curl around the base of the bucket handle and trim. Repeat on the other side.

5 Use the template (see page 123), or draw a leaf shape on cardboard, and cut it out. Draw around the cardboard shape on colored construction paper and cut out lots of leaf shapes. Score the leaf pattern onto the leaves using the sharp end of the scissors and a ruler, and bend the leaves slightly to make them look more three-dimensional.

6 Glue the paper leaves around the bucket, varying the angles and overlapping them slightly. Continue around the bucket until all the leaves are stuck on.

peg-doll fairy

This fairy is very special and therefore you will need to buy some very special materials to make her——but it will be worth it when you see her shining and magical at the top of the Christmas tree.

You will need:

☆☆☆☆☆☆☆☆☆☆☆

A round wooden clothespin

Acrylic paints for her skin and hair

A fine paintbrush

A fine marker pen

Gold organza

Scissors, needle, and thread

PVA glue

24 in. (60 cm) of 1½-in. (35-mm) wide gold organza ribbon

A flower sequin for her hair

A star sequin and string of tiny sequins for the wand

Gold sequins

Ribbon about 16 in. (40 cm) long

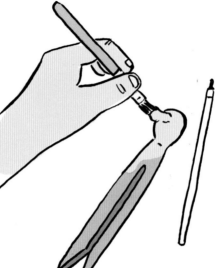

1 Paint the top of the clothespin with flesh-colored paint. When it is dry, paint on the hair and draw on the eyes and mouth with a fine pen.

2 Cut two pieces of organza, each measuring 9 x 4 in. (22 x 10 cm). Thread your needle. Lay one piece of organza on top of the other and, close to the top edge, sew a few stitches to stop the thread from pulling through. Then sew running stitches (see page 119) along the top through both layers. Pull the thread to gather up the material (see page 121), making sure that it fits around the clothespin. Finish with a few stitches to hold the gathers in place.

3 Wrap the skirt around the clothespin and stitch it together at the back. A dab of glue will help to hold it in place. Leave the glue to dry.

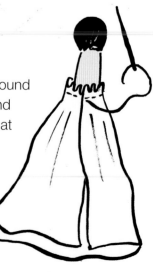

4 Fold the gold ribbon in half lengthwise. Dab glue around the body of the clothespin and wrap the ribbon around it, tying it at the back. Leave it to dry. Open out the rest of the ribbon and cut the ends into a V-shape.

5 Tie the ribbon into a big bow to look like wings.

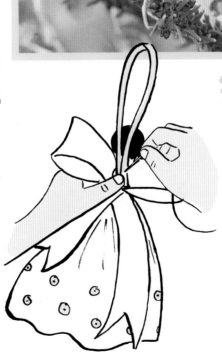

6 Finish off by using the sequins. Glue a flower sequin to the hair. Make a wand from the string of tiny sequins and a star sequin, and glue it in place. Glue gold sequins onto the skirt. Stitch a ribbon to the back of the fairy, so that you can tie her to the tree.

salt-dough gingerbread man

This year, why not top your Christmas tree with a gingerbread man who looks as if he's just escaped from a story book? He is made out of salt dough, baked hard, painted, and then finished off with buttons and rickrack glued around the edge to look like icing. After you have cut him out, there will be enough salt dough to make all sorts of other decorations to hang on your tree.

You will need:

For the salt dough:

A mixing bowl

A wooden spoon

Kitchen scales

A measuring cup

Measuring spoons

5 oz (150 g) salt

3½ fl. oz (100 ml) lukewarm water

5 oz (150 g) flour

½ tablespoon vegetable oil

Gingerbread man cookie cutter

Other cookie cutters

Baking tray

For the gingerbread man decorations:

Brown acrylic paint and paintbrush

40 in. (1 metre) white rickrack braid

Scissors

PVA glue

2 black buttons

3 white buttons

Small piece of red felt for mouth

10 in. (25 cm) ribbon for bow

20 in. (50 cm) ribbon for ties

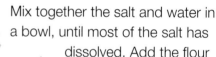

1 Mix together the salt and water in a bowl, until most of the salt has dissolved. Add the flour and oil and mix together to form a dough that is soft enough to roll out. You can start by using a spoon, but your hands are the best tools for this. Add more water if the dough is too crumbly or more flour if it is too sticky.

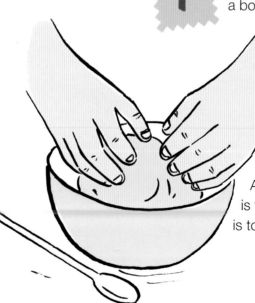

2 Sprinkle flour onto the work surface and roll the dough out to a thickness of about ½ in. (1.5 cm). Cut out the gingerbread man and place him on the baking tray. Cut out other shapes with the left-over dough, gathering the bits together and rolling it out again.

3 Set the oven to 200°F (100°C/Gas Mark ¼). Put the tray of shapes into the oven. Check the dough after about an hour to see if it is hard. It may need slightly longer—if so, leave it in the oven and check it every ten minutes. When it's ready, turn off the heat and leave it in the oven to cool.

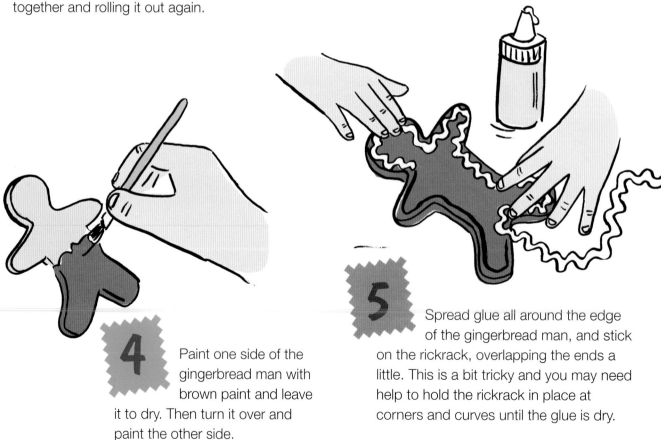

4 Paint one side of the gingerbread man with brown paint and leave it to dry. Then turn it over and paint the other side.

5 Spread glue all around the edge of the gingerbread man, and stick on the rickrack, overlapping the ends a little. This is a bit tricky and you may need help to hold the rickrack in place at corners and curves until the glue is dry.

6

Glue on black button eyes and a red felt mouth. Stick three white buttons down the middle of the gingerbread man's tummy, and a bow at his neck. Leave the glue to dry completely.

7

You will need to stick ribbons to the back of the gingerbread man so that you can tie him to the top of the tree. Cut two pieces of ribbon, each about 10 in. (25 cm) long, and stick them to his back. Leave to dry.

Tip

Salt dough is very easy to make and use, but needs to be "cooked" at a very low temperature so that it does not crack. Leave the salt-dough decorations in the oven until they are completely cold to stop them from cracking as they cool.

You will need:

For the cookies:

1 cup (200 g) butter

½ cup (100 g) superfine (caster) sugar

3 cups (450 g) all-purpose (plain) flour

½ teaspoon baking powder

1 extra-large (large UK) egg

1 teaspoon vanilla extract

A set of Christmas cookie cutters

2 baking trays

Baking parchment

Plastic wrap (cling film)

For the icing:

1 cup (200 g) confectioners' (icing) sugar

Red, green, and yellow food coloring

A pack of colored writing icing tubes

Silver cake decorating balls

A pack of mini marshmallows

Cellophane bags and ribbons (optional)

3 plastic bowls

christmas cookies

These cookies are pretty, delicious, and fun to make. For a finishing touch, wrap them in cellophane bags with ribbon ties or else present them in a pile on a beautiful plate. **Remember** to ask an adult to help you with the cooking. The easiest way to make these cookies is in a food processor, but you could mix them by hand. Be sure to take your butter out of the fridge an hour or so before you start, so that it is nice and soft.

1 Put on an apron and wash your hands well with soap and warm water. Preheat the oven to 350°F (180°C/Gas 4). Line the baking trays with baking parchment and rub the butter wrapper lightly over the top. This will stop the cookies from sticking to the parchment.

2 In the food processor or a large mixing bowl, mix together the butter, sugar, flour, baking powder, egg, and vanilla extract and form into a dough ball.

Homemade *DECORATIONS you can* **EAT** *are the best!*

3 Divide the dough ball into four pieces, wrap each piece in plastic wrap (cling film), then put in the fridge to cool for about an hour.

4 Sprinkle some flour on your work surface and roll out the first piece of dough until it is about ¼ in. (6 mm) thick. Cut out Christmas shapes using the cookie cutters and lift them carefully onto the baking trays. Collect together all the trimmings, roll them out again, and cut out more shapes. Do the same with the other pieces of dough.

6 Sift the confectioners' (icing) sugar into a bowl and add about two tablespoons of water. Stir the mixture adding a little more water, one teaspoon at a time, until the icing is smooth and runny enough to drip off the spoon. Divide the icing into three bowls and color each one with a different food coloring.

5 Place the trays in the oven for 6 minutes until the edges of the shapes are just beginning to turn golden. Be careful not to burn them. Allow the cookies to cool on their trays for a few minutes before transferring them to the cooling rack.

7 Decorate your cookies using the icing, writing icing, edible balls, and mini marshmallows. Use your imagination to make them beautiful, or follow the photo above for ideas.

CLOCKWISE, FROM LEFT:

☆ A red heart iced into the center of the cookie can be sparkled up with silver balls.

☆ Give sheep a woolly look by icing in white then adding mini marshmallows for a fleece.

☆ The little angel looks gorgeous in her pink dress! Use writing icing to give her curly blonde hair, dark eyes, and red rosebud lips.

☆ Ice Rudolph's body red to match his nose.

☆ Ice Christmas trees in green and use silver balls to decorate.

☆ Make stars special by icing in white, then using yellow writing icing to draw out a star shape on top.

sewing techniques

The best way to learn something new is to ask someone to teach you. Is there someone in your family who can sew? If there is, they will probably be very pleased to pass on their skills. If not, follow the instructions below. All the sewing techniques in this book are easy to learn and do.

How to use a pattern

There are lots of templates in this book to help you make patterns for the projects. To use them:

1 Trace the template onto tracing paper or thin paper which you can see through and cut them out to make a pattern.

2 Pin this pattern onto your fabric, making sure that the fabric is flat with no creases. Position the pattern close to the edges of the fabric so that you don't waste any. If you need two pieces that are the same shape, fold the fabric over and pin the pattern so the pins go through both layers.

3 If the pattern has a dotted fold line on it, fold the fabric over and pin the pattern piece onto it, positioning the fold line on the pattern along the fold of the fabric. Cut around the pattern as close to the edge as you can.

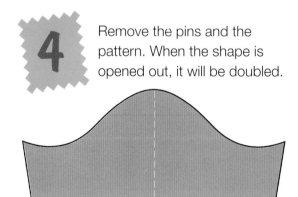

4 Remove the pins and the pattern. When the shape is opened out, it will be doubled.

How to use half-size templates

A few templates, which are marked as "half-size," need to be doubled in size to make the pattern big enough. The easiest way to do this is to ask somebody to photocopy the template for you using the 200% zoom button on the photocopier.

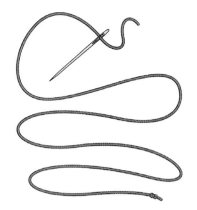

Threading a needle

1 Thread your needle with about 25 in (65 cm) of thread or yarn (wool). Pull about 6 in (15 cm) of the thread through the needle. Tie two knots on top of each other at the other end.

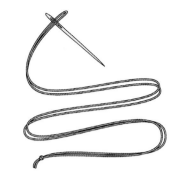

2 For a double thread, which is stronger, pull the thread through the needle until the thread is doubled over and tie a knot in the two ends together.

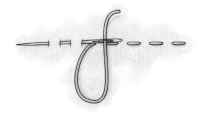

Running stitch

This is the simplest stitch and can be used in embroidery and for joining two layers of fabric together. It is very easy to do but not very strong.

Secure the end of the thread with a few small stitches. Push the needle down through the fabric a little way along, then bring it back up through the fabric a little way along. Repeat to form a row of stitches.

Finishing stitching

It is important to finish off all your stitching so that it doesn't come undone.

When you have finished stitching, sew a few tiny stitches over and over in the same place on the back of the fabric. Then trim off your thread.

Backstitch

This is a very useful stitch as it is strong and similar to the stitches used on a sewing machine. It makes a solid line of stitches.

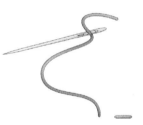

1 Start as if you were sewing running stitch. Sew one stitch and bring the needle back up to start the second stitch.

2 This time, instead of going forward, go back and push the needle through at the end of your first stitch.

3 Bring it out again a stitch length past the thread. Keep going to make an even line of stitches with no gaps.

Blanket stitch

This makes a pretty edge when you are sewing two layers of felt together.

1 Bring the needle through at the edge of the fabric.

2 Push the needle back through the fabric a short distance from the edge and loop the thread under the needle. Pull the needle and thread as far as you can to make the first stitch.

3 Make another stitch to the right of this and again loop the thread under the needle. Continue along the fabric and finish with a few small stitches or a knot on the underside.

Stem stitch

This stitch is used to embroider patterns, especially to make lines of pretty stitching.

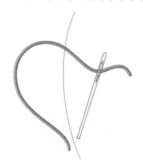

1 Draw a line where you want your stitching to be.

2 Pull the needle up through the fabric a little to the left of the line. Push it down a little to the right of the line and a bit further up to make a diagonal stitch.

3 Pull it up again next to your first stitch and continue like this. Try to keep your stitches the size and at the same angle.

Stuffing

1 When you sew up a stuffed toy, leave a small gap for the stuffing. Leave the thread loose and take off the needle, while you do the stuffing.

2 Push small pieces of stuffing into the toy and use a pencil to push the stuffing into the furthest places first, especially narrow spaces like arms, legs, and ears.

3 Pack the stuffing quite firmly. When you have finished, thread your needle again and sew up the gap. Finish with a few small finishing stitches.

Sewing on a button

1 Mark the place where you want the button.

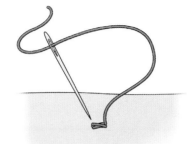

2 Push the needle up from the back of the fabric and sew a few stitches over and over in this place.

3 Now bring the needle up through one of the holes in the button. Push the needle back down through the second hole and through the fabric. Bring it back up through the first hole. Repeat this five or six times. If there are four holes in the button use all four of them to make a cross pattern. Make sure that you keep the stitches close together under the middle of the button.

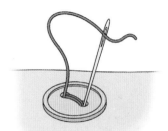

4 Finish with a few small stitches over and over on the back of the fabric and trim the thread.

Gathering

1 To gather a piece of fabric, knot your thread and begin with a few small stitches over and over in the same place on the fabric to hold the thread firmly so it won't pull through.

2 Now sew a line of running stitches—the smaller the stitches, the smaller the gathers you will make.

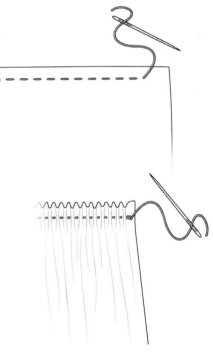

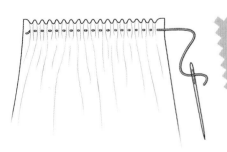

3 At the end, don't finish off; leave the thread loose. Pull the fabric back along the line of stitches so it gathers up into folds.

4 When it is the right size, secure the end of the thread with a few stitches over and over in the same place so the fabric can't come ungathered.

Templates

For instructions on how to use these templates, see page 118.

PAPIER-MÂCHÉ MASKS

(page 66)

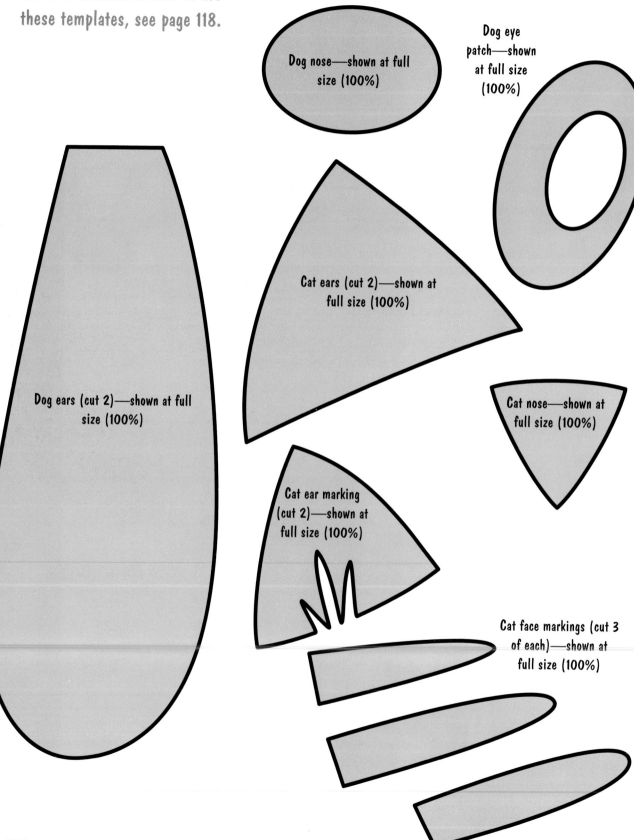

Dog nose—shown at full size (100%)

Dog eye patch—shown at full size (100%)

Cat ears (cut 2)—shown at full size (100%)

Dog ears (cut 2)—shown at full size (100%)

Cat nose—shown at full size (100%)

Cat ear marking (cut 2)—shown at full size (100%)

Cat face markings (cut 3 of each)—shown at full size (100%)

PIRATE HAT AND EYE PATCH

(page 74)

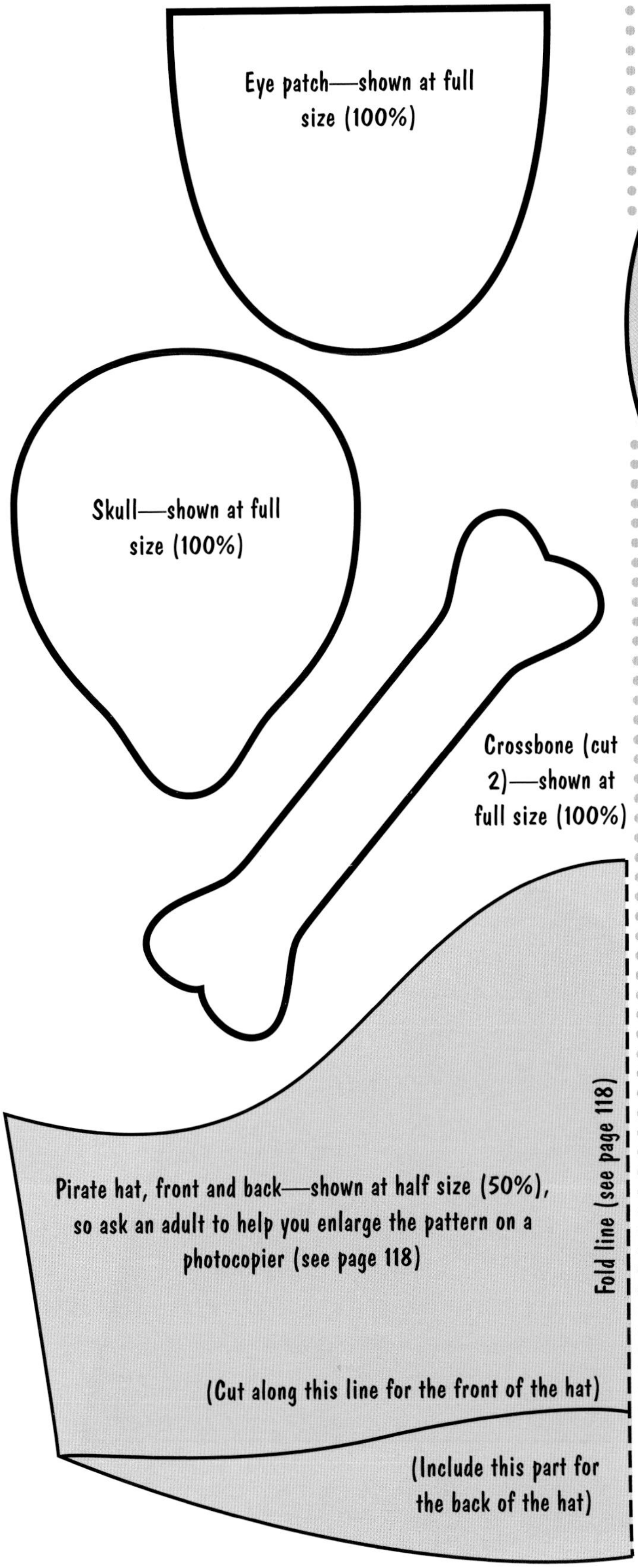

Eye patch—shown at full size (100%)

Skull—shown at full size (100%)

Crossbone (cut 2)—shown at full size (100%)

Pirate hat, front and back—shown at half size (50%), so ask an adult to help you enlarge the pattern on a photocopier (see page 118)

Fold line (see page 118)

(Cut along this line for the front of the hat)

(Include this part for the back of the hat)

LADYBUG PINCUSHION

(page 46)

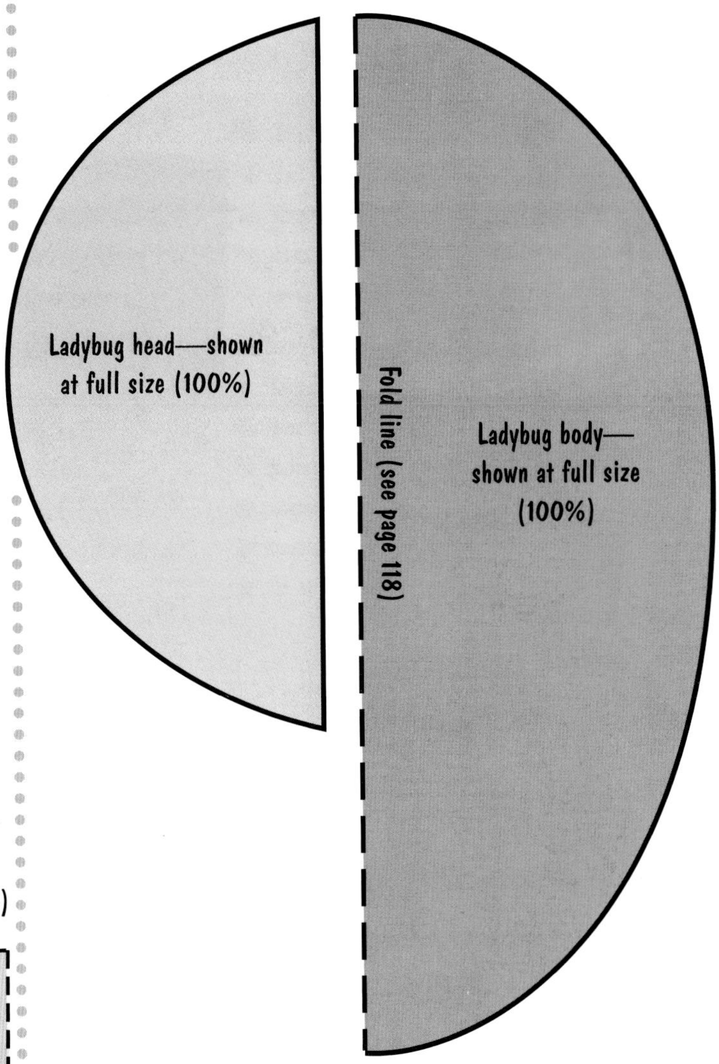

Ladybug head—shown at full size (100%)

Fold line (see page 118)

Ladybug body—shown at full size (100%)

TRICK-OR-TREAT BASKET

(page 106)

Leaf shape—shown at full size (100%)

TEDDY BEAR
(page 52)

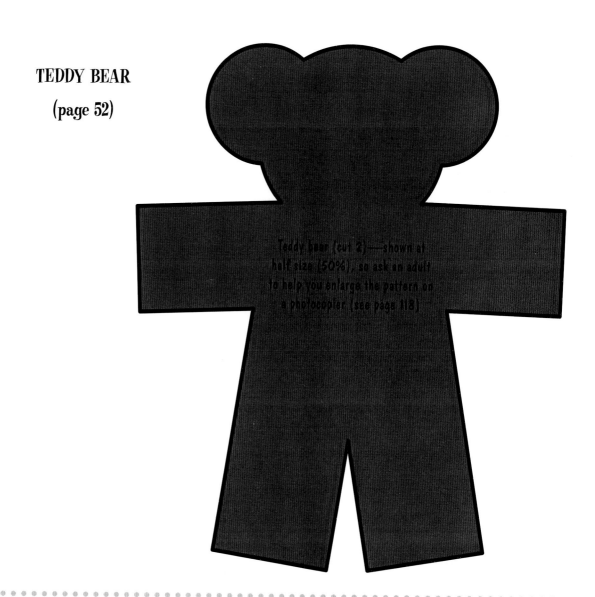

Teddy bear (cut 2)—shown at half size (50%), so ask an adult to help you enlarge the pattern on a photocopier (see page 118)

CHICKEN EGG COZY
(page 54)

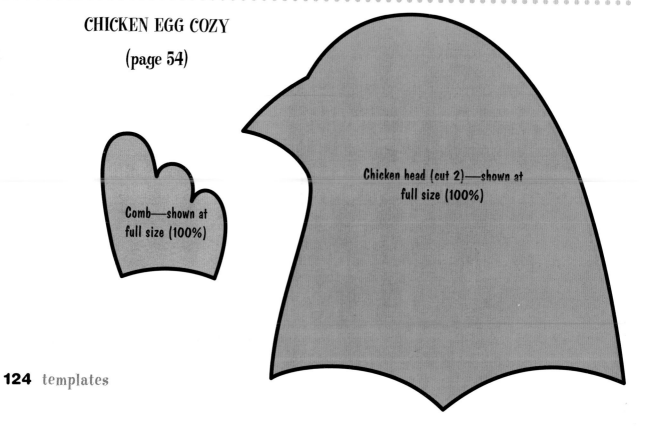

Comb—shown at full size (100%)

Chicken head (cut 2)—shown at full size (100%)

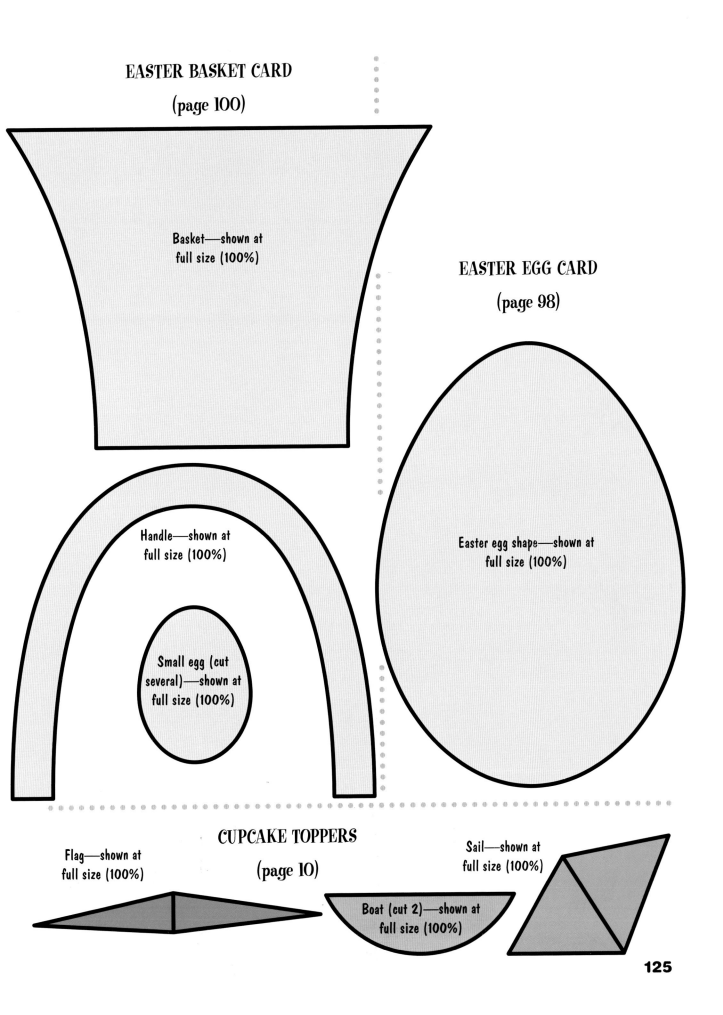

EASTER BASKET CARD

(page 100)

Basket—shown at full size (100%)

EASTER EGG CARD

(page 98)

Handle—shown at full size (100%)

Easter egg shape—shown at full size (100%)

Small egg (cut several)—shown at full size (100%)

CUPCAKE TOPPERS

(page 10)

Flag—shown at full size (100%)

Sail—shown at full size (100%)

Boat (cut 2)—shown at full size (100%)

ANIMAL HATS
(page 70)

ROYAL CROWNS
(page 78)

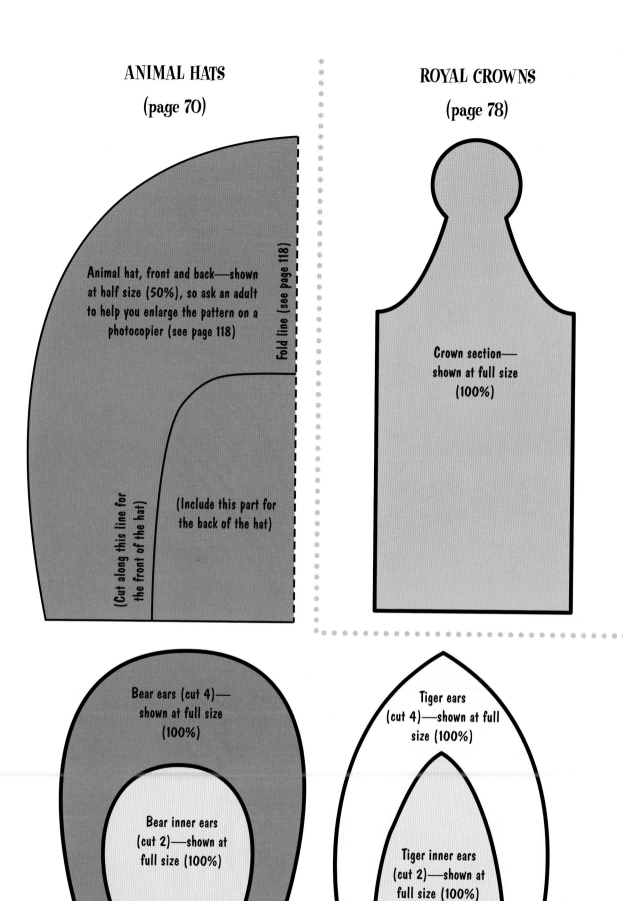

Animal hat, front and back—shown at half size (50%), so ask an adult to help you enlarge the pattern on a photocopier (see page 118)

Fold line (see page 118)

(Cut along this line for the front of the hat)

(Include this part for the back of the hat)

Crown section—shown at full size (100%)

Bear ears (cut 4)—shown at full size (100%)

Bear inner ears (cut 2)—shown at full size (100%)

Tiger ears (cut 4)—shown at full size (100%)

Tiger inner ears (cut 2)—shown at full size (100%)

FLOWER FAIRY

(page 30)

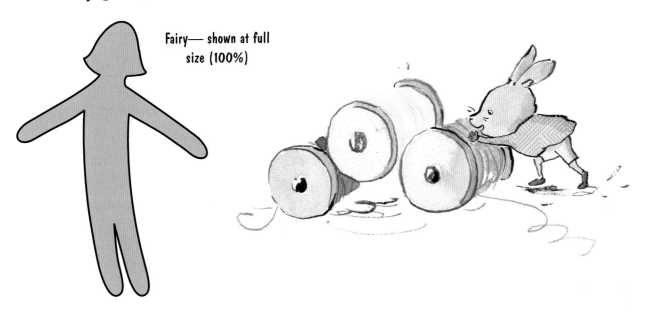

Fairy— shown at full size (100%)

Suppliers

US

A C Moore
www.acmoore.com

The Baker's Kitchen
www.thebakerskitchen.net

Create For Less
www.createforless.com

Creative Kids Crafts
www.creativekidscrafts.com

Darice
www.darice.com

Hobby Lobby
www.hobbylobby.com

Jo-ann Fabric & Crafts
www.joann.com

Michaels
www.michaels.com

UK

Early Learning Centre
www.elc.co.uk

Homecrafts Direct
www.homecrafts.co.uk

Hobbycraft
www.hobbycraft.co.uk

John Lewis
www.johnlewis.co.uk

Lakeland
www.lakeland.co.uk

Letterbox
www.letterbox.co.uk

Paperchase
www.paperchase.co.uk

Woolworths
www.woolworths.co.uk

Index

Numbers in **bold** refer to templates.

Acknowledgments

Project makers
Linda Collister: 86–89, 92–95
Tessa Evelegh: 114-117
Emma Hardy: 12–17, 22–23, 26–41, 44–49,
58–79, 98–103, 106–113
Mari Ono: 18–21
Annie Rigg: 84–85, 90–91
Deborah Schneebeli-Morrell: 50–51, 54–55,
104–105
Christina Strutt: 52–53
Nicki Trench: 82–83
Clare Youngs: 10–11

Photography
L = left, R = right, T = top, B = bottom

Caroline Arber: 115, 177
Carolyn Barber: 5T, 19, 21,
Terry Benson: 5B, 56, 59, 61, 79
Vanessa Davies: 1R, 7b, 80, 87, 93
Winfried Heinze: 6, 83
Lisa Linder: 81, 85, 91
Gloria Nicol: 107
Debbie Patterson: 1L, 2–4, 7T, 8, 17, 23, 24,
25, 27–29, 31, 33, 35, 37, 39–43, 45, 47, 49,
57, 63–65, 67–69, 70–73, 75, 77, 96, 109,
111, 113
Claire Richardson: 9, 11
Heini Schneebeli: 51, 55, 97, 105
Tino Tedaldi: 13, 99, 101
Edina van der Wyck: 53

Jacket photography: back cover: Tino Tedaldi
(T), Vanessa Davies (R), Terry Benson (B);
spine and front cover main image: Debbie
Patterson; front cover insets, Lisa Linder (TL)
and Debbie Patterson (R, B).